Key Issues in Network Protocols and Security

Edited by Mamata Rath and Tusharkanta Samal

Published in London, United Kingdom

Key Issues in Network Protocols and Security
http://dx.doi.org/10.5772/intechopen.1004498
Edited by Mamata Rath and Tusharkanta Samal

Contributors
Danial Yousef, Daniel R. Garcia Avila, Jan van den Berg, Jerry F. Miller, Jose Antonio Gazquez, Kenneth Wong, Maher Abur-rous, Mamata Rath, Mohamad Al-Samhouri, Nuria Novas, Sundararaj S. Iyengar

First published in London, United Kingdom, 2025 by IntechOpen
IntechOpen is the global imprint of INTECHOPEN LIMITED, registered in England and Wales, registration number: 11086078, 167-169 Great Portland Street, London, W1W 5PF, United Kingdom

For EU product safety concerns: IN TECH d.o.o., Prolaz Marije Krucifikse Kozulić 3, 51000 Rijeka, Croatia, info@intechopen.com or visit our website at intechopen.com.

British Library Cataloguing-in-Publication Data
A catalogue record for this book is available from the British Library

Key Issues in Network Protocols and Security
Edited by Mamata Rath and Tusharkanta Samal
p. cm.
Print ISBN 978-1-83634-335-6
Online ISBN 978-1-83634-334-9
eBook (PDF) ISBN 978-1-83634-336-3

If disposing of this product, please recycle the paper responsibly.

Meet the editors

Dr. Mamata Rath is working as an associate professor of computer science and engineering at GITA Autonomous College Bhubaneswar in India. She has completed a Ph.D. in Computer Science from S. O. A. University, India and an M. Tech (Comp. Sc) from the College of Engineering & Technology, Bhubaneswar, India, under Biju Patnaik University of Technology (BPUT). Her research interests are machine learning, big data analytics, data mining, wireless Ad-hoc networks, VANET, Internet of Things (IoT) and computer security. She has many research publications indexed in Scopus and Web of Science. Her research articles have been published in the *Defense Science Journal, Elsevier, Emerald, IEEE,* and *Wiley*, to name a few. She has edited several books for various international publishers. The subjects of the books are emerging topics like resource management in networks, artificial intelligence and computational modeling in COVID-19 research. She is a regular reviewer of research papers for *Wiley* and *Elsevier.*

Dr. Tusharkanta Samal is an Associate Professor in the Department of Computer Science and Engineering, SOET, at DRIEMS University, India. He earned his B. Tech from DRIEMS and M. Tech and Ph.D. from the Veer Surendra Sai University of Technology in Burla, India. With over 8 years of teaching experience and more than 5 years of research experience, he has published over 30 articles in international journals and conferences. Dr. Samal has also qualified for the GATE and UGC NET exams conducted by the Government of India. Currently, he also serves as the Professor in Charge of the Ph.D. Cell at DRIEMS University.

Contents

Preface

The importance of energetic network protocols and security mechanisms cannot be overstated in an era where digital connectivity shapes our daily lives. From personal communications to critical infrastructure, the internet underpins almost every aspect of modern society. *Key Issues in Network Protocols and Security* explores the fundamental problems and advancements that propel the growth and protection of modern networks. This book aims to provide readers with a comprehensive understanding of the principles and practices that govern network communication and security in research. It examines fundamental concepts, explores emerging technologies, and addresses real-world problems network professionals and researchers face. The subjects covered are protocol design, performance optimization, encryption standards, intrusion detection, and the changing nature of cyber threats.

This book is intended for academic and investigative audiences and was written with fresh research concepts. It is an invaluable resource for engineers, engineering students, and cybersecurity professionals wishing to learn more about this dynamic sector. Special emphasis has been placed on blending theoretical foundations with practical applications, ensuring readers can translate insights into actionable solutions.

The Introductory Chapter by the editor titled "Navigating the Complexities of Network Protocols and Security" focuses on modern threats, highlighting the flaws in network architecture, including cyber attacks, data breaches, and unauthorized access. The growth of technologies like cloud computing, 5G networks, and the Internet of Things (IoT) adds new degrees of complexity and exacerbates these risks. Finding a balance between security, interoperability, and efficiency has become more difficult for developers and organizations in critical networking environments. In-depth discussions of network protocols and security are covered in this chapter, along with their flaws, evolving threats, and risk-reduction strategies. By examining practical issues and creative solutions, it aims to provide a comprehensive understanding of this critical and ever-evolving subject. Whether you are an IT specialist, researcher, or student, this inquiry equips you with the knowledge you need to comprehend network protocols and safeguard digital infrastructures.

The chapter, "Current Challenges in IoT Security and Forensics: Strategies for a Secure Connected Future", by Daniel R. Garcia Avila, Jerry F. Miller and Sundararaj S. Iyengar demonstrates that the exponential growth of the Internet of Things (IoT) has introduced considerable security and forensic challenges due to the rising complexity and heterogeneity of connected devices. As the adoption of the Internet of Things (IoT) continues to expand, so do the vulnerabilities inherent to this technology, with threats ranging from exploiting individual devices to large-scale network security breaches. IoT security frameworks must evolve continuously to address cryptography, authentication, and communication protocol weaknesses. Concurrently, the field of IoT forensics encounters obstacles in the gathering and analysis of evidence due to the restricted memory and heterogeneous architectures of IoT devices. This chapter examines the critical aspects of IoT security, highlighting prevalent attacks, mitigation techniques, and the forensic methodologies employed to investigate compromised devices. Particular attention is given to device heterogeneity, emerging forensic tools, and artificial intelligence's impact on security and forensic efforts. The discussion underscores the necessity for ongoing advancements to create a resilient IoT ecosystem capable of mitigating threats and enhancing forensic investigations.

The next chapter is "Post-Quantum Cryptography for Wireless Sensor Network Using Key Agreement Super Singular on Hyperelliptic Curve" by Mohamad Al-Samhouri, Nuria Novas, Maher Abur-rous and Jose Antonio Gazquez. The intersection of security and sustainability within wireless sensor networks (WSNs) underscores pivotal factors such as energy efficiency, resource optimization, energy waste reduction, and the sustained integrity of network infrastructure. This interplay ensures that deployments are not just efficient but also ecologically sound. WSNs comprise autonomously dispersed sensors linked to battery-powered devices, facilitating wireless data transmission. The optimization of WSNs through Fog and Edge Computing signifies a paradigm shift, diminishing reliance on central cloud servers. This adaptive strategy enhances WSN efficiency across diverse environmental conditions by streamlining data transmission to centralized cloud servers. In cryptographic systems, conventional approaches reliant on mathematical algorithms to secure communication channels encounter vulnerabilities. Quantum cryptography presents a more robust alternative to conventional methods, while post-quantum cryptography (PQC) employs algorithms resilient to both traditional and quantum threats. This chapter introduces a novel approach for mutual authentication and generating session keys in communications between WSN nodes. Authors use super singular Hyperelliptic Curve Cryptography (HECC) with a small size by exchanging key Diffie-Hellman (DH) to improve security in IoT and WSN. This method provides a promising mix of quantum resistance and integration into conventional approaches.

The next chapter is "Innovative Vision Glasses for Glaucoma Detection and Management" by Kenneth Wong. The creation and use of novel vision glasses designed to measure intraocular pressure (IOP), a critical component of glaucoma monitoring and treatment, are examined in this report. These advanced glasses integrate multiple embedded sensors to offer continuous, real-time data on critical ocular health metrics, facilitating early detection and more effective management of glaucoma. The glasses are equipped with pressure sensors to monitor IOP, focus sensors to evaluate visual acuity, temperature sensors to detect signs of inflammation, and blue light sensors to measure exposure to potentially harmful light. All these components are seamlessly integrated with a microcontroller and a wireless communication system for efficient data transmission and processing. The adoption of this technology promises significant benefits, including increased patient convenience, enhanced accessibility to eye care, and improved early detection capabilities. Moreover, the report features a Python script designed to simulate the glasses' functionality, monitor various parameters, and process data to generate alerts based on predefined thresholds. Looking ahead, the report explores future advancements and broader applications in ophthalmology, such as personalized treatment plans and integration with electronic health records, emphasizing the transformative potential of this technology in advancing eye care and glaucoma management.

The chapter "Unveiling the Stealthy Threat: Low-Rate Denial of Service (LDoS) Attacks" by Danial Yousef discusses Low-Rate Denial of Service (LDoS) attacks, which differ from traditional Denial of Service (DoS) attacks by subtly exploiting the internet's Transmission Control Protocol (TCP) to degrade network performance. LDoS attacks send small amounts of traffic at strategic times, making them hard to detect, especially if the timing is random. The chapter explains these attacks and their detection methods, from early frequency domain analysis to advanced machine learning and Software-Defined Networking (SDN) techniques. It aims to provide a comprehensive understanding of LDoS attacks, their mechanisms, and detection strategies, highlighting the ongoing efforts to combat this critical cyber security challenge.

The chapter titled "Present-Day Cybersecurity: Actual Challenges and Solution Directions" by Jan van den Berg communicates that currently available cyberspace services offer all kinds of possibilities for individuals, businesses, and organizations to arrange their lives and improve their e-enabled business processes. However, next to the numerous benefits, people are aware of many less desirable developments in cyberspace. In other words, the security of cyberspace (i.e., cyber security) is at stake, and we have to act in this (relatively new) domain. In this chapter, the authors first provide a condensed overview of existing and upcoming cyber activities and cyber processes in various cyber subdomains, using holistic cyberspace model terminology. The authors also introduce a general cyber risk management model. Next, they present an overview of a series of (mostly) recent cyber incidents, based on which we formulate related cyber security challenges. To understand how we currently deal with these challenges, they describe the current efforts of various cyberspace actors to enhance cyber-security to a sufficient resilience level and evaluate the limitations of their endeavors. By putting together all findings, researchers conclude an overview of actual cyber security solution directions, that is, an overview of the efforts needed to bring security in all cyberspace subdomains to acceptable levels.

The journey to edit this book has been both challenging and rewarding. We thank the contributors and reviewers whose expertise has shaped its content. We hope this book inspires innovation and strengthens the resilience of global networks in the face of dynamic threats.

We invite readers to engage with the material, challenge assumptions, and contribute to the ongoing discourse on network protocols and security.

Dr. Mamata Rath
Associate Professor (CSE),
GITA Autonomous College,
India

Dr. Tusharakanta Samal
Associate Professor (CSE),
DRIEMS University,
Cuttack, India

Chapter 1

Introductory Chapter: Navigating the Complexities of Network Protocols and Security

Mamata Rath

1. Introduction

Network protocols and security are the foundation of digital communication in today's hyper-connected society. These protocols provide smooth communication between devices, apps, and systems by defining the guidelines for data exchange across networks. However, the difficulties in creating and sustaining secure protocols have grown more complex as networks get bigger and more sophisticated [1].

Cyberattacks, data breaches, and un-authorised access are examples of contemporary risks that draw attention to the weaknesses in network architecture. These dangers are made worse by the development of technologies such as cloud computing, 5G networks, and the Internet of Things (IoT), which add new levels of complexity [2]. In a critical networking environment, for both developers and organisations, striking a balance between security, interoperability, and efficiency has grown increasingly challenging and difficult.

This discussion dives into the important topics of network protocols and security, examining the weaknesses, changing dangers, and risk-reduction techniques. It seeks to offer a thorough grasp of this vital and dynamic topic by looking at real-world problems and innovative solutions [3]. Regardless of your background—researcher, IT specialist, or enthusiast this investigation gives you the knowledge you need to understand network protocols and protect digital infrastructures.

2. Challenges in secured protocol design in networking

Creating secure network protocols is a complex task that calls for striking a careful balance between resilience against a constantly changing threat landscape, performance, and functionality. Ensuring end-to-end security without sacrificing network efficiency is one of the main challenges. Protocols must ensure low latency and high throughput while protecting data from interception, manipulation, and un-authorised access. Trade-offs between encryption strength, computational overhead, and compatibility with current infrastructure are frequently necessary to achieve this balance [4]. Furthermore, supporting a broad range of platforms and devices adds to the challenge of upholding uniform security requirements as networks grow more diverse.

The quick development of cyber threats is another significant obstacle. Attackers constantly take advantage of flaws in current protocols, requiring frequent redesigns and modifications. For example, outdated protocols like FTP or HTTP, which were first created with little regard for security, frequently turn into vulnerabilities in contemporary networks. Furthermore, new vulnerabilities brought about by the integration of future technologies like IoT, 5G, and edge computing include the restricted processing power of IoT devices, which may limit the implementation of robust encryption methods [5]. The problem is made worse by the absence of global security standards in these areas, which makes it challenging to apply and enforce uniform procedures across various ecosystems. As a result, developing safe protocols requires not just technical know-how but also a vision to foresee potential risks and flexibility to proactively counter them.

3. Resolution of confronts in secured protocol design in networking

Addressing the complexities of secured protocol design in networking requires a combination of innovative technologies, best practices, and collaborative efforts across industries [6]. Below are actionable solutions to the challenges outlined.

Use cutting-edge encryption standards (such as RSA and AES-256) to safeguard the confidentiality and integrity of data. For devices with limited resources, like the Internet of Things, use lightweight encryption algorithms. To get ready for the arrival of quantum computing, implement cryptographic approaches that are resistant to quantum errors. Create modular protocols that enable patches and upgrades without interfering with network functionality. Make use of security measures that are adaptable to changing network sizes and traffic volumes. Use software-defined networking (SDN) to allow for dynamic protocol behaviour modifications [7].

3.1 Fortifying authorisation and authentication systems

To strengthen identity verification, implement multi-factor authentication (MFA).

For digital signatures and safe key exchange, make use of public key infrastructure (PKI).

To dynamically restrict privileges, use role-based and context-aware access controls.

To find and fix possible flaws, perform regular vulnerability assessments.

Use fuzz testing to assess how resilient the protocol is to erroneous inputs.

Prove protocol security properties mathematically using formal verification techniques.

3.2 Standardising security procedures

Work together across sectors to create and implement industry-wide security standards for cutting-edge technologies like 5G and the Internet of Things.

Encourage the adoption of open standards for secure communication, such as TLS, HTTPS, and IPsec.

Provide standards for the safe creation and implementation of protocols.

Slowly replace insecure protocols like HTTP and FTP with more secure ones like HTTPS and SFTP. Introduce safe additions to legacy systems while maintaining backward compatibility. Use tunnelling or protocol wrappers to contain vulnerable protocols inside.

3.3 Making use of AI and machine learning

Use machine learning algorithms to identify and react to unusual traffic patterns that could be signs of danger. To anticipate such weaknesses and suggest preventative actions, use AI-driven technologies. To speed up response times, automate threat analysis and patching procedures [8]. Educate developers and network engineers on protocol design concepts and safe coding techniques. To keep experts abreast of the most recent dangers and solutions, offer frequent training and certifications. Encourage industry-academia cooperation to advance secure protocol design research and innovation [9].

3.4 Using redundancy to build resilience

To guarantee continuation in the event of an attack, provide redundancy and failover methods in the protocol design. For safe and impenetrable data transfers, use distributed systems such as blockchain [10]. Put disaster recovery strategies and routine backups into action. Integrate privacy-preserving elements into protocols, like anonymisation and data minimisation. Integrate privacy standards to guarantee adherence to international laws such as GDPR and HIPAA. Give users authority over access rights and data sharing.

4. Using machine learning approach in secured communication and networking

Machine learning (ML) has become a game-changing technique for improving networking and communication system security. Networks can greatly increase overall security by using ML algorithms to identify and react to cyber threats instantly. To categorise harmful activity in network traffic, supervised learning methods like support vector machines and decision trees are frequently employed. Unsupervised learning methods, such as anomaly detection and grouping, are useful for spotting unidentified security risks. Deep learning models, such as recurrent neural networks (RNNs) and convolutional neural networks (CNNs), offer sophisticated skills for deciphering intricate network patterns. ML-based intrusion detection systems (IDS) have a high degree of accuracy in differentiating between malicious and benign activity. Reinforcement learning is being used to adjust to changing threats and optimise dynamic network security rules. By guaranteeing safe key exchange and authentication procedures, machine learning algorithms improve the efficacy of encryption techniques. ML helps identify and prevent distributed denial-of-service (DDoS) and man-in-the-middle (MITM) attacks in secure communication. Machine learning (ML) techniques are crucial for protecting Internet of Things (IoT) devices, whose low computational capabilities make them susceptible to cyberattacks. During security crises, real-time threat intelligence produced by machine learning models facilitates quicker decision-making and shorter response times. Federated learning guarantees that machine learning models can be trained on dispersed devices without sacrificing.

5. Conclusion

Secured protocol design difficulties can be successfully solved by implementing a multifaceted strategy that incorporates cutting-edge technologies, ongoing testing, and teamwork. These solutions guarantee the security and dependability of digital communication in a world that is growing more interconnected by strengthening the resilience of contemporary networks and preparing them for potential threats.

Author details

Mamata Rath
GITA Autonomous College, India

*Address all correspondence to: mamata.rath200@gmail.com

References

[1] Shim KS, Sohn I, Lee E, Seok W, Lee W. Enhance the ICS network security using the whitelist-based network monitoring through protocol analysis. Journal of Web Engineering. 2021;**20**(1):1-32. DOI: 10.13052/jwe1540-9589.2011

[2] Wang X, Ma J. Cloud-network-end collaborative security for wireless networks: Architecture, mechanisms, and applications. Tsinghua Science and Technology. 2025;**30**(1):18-33. DOI: 10.26599/TST.2023.9010158

[3] Saleem MA, Shamshad S, Ahmed S, Ghaffar Z, Mahmood K. Security analysis on "A secure three-factor user authentication protocol with forward secrecy for wireless medical sensor network systems". IEEE Systems Journal. 2021;**15**(4):5557-5559. DOI: 10.1109/JSYST.2021.3073537

[4] Madoery PG, Cherini R, Cammarano A, Grosso J, Finochietto JM. Bundle protocol security models and policies for safeguarding space information networks. IEEE Journal of Radio Frequency Identification. 2024;**8**:547-558. DOI: 10.1109/JRFID.2024.3406890

[5] Fernandez L, Karlsson G. Black-box fuzzing for security in managed networks: An outline. IEEE Networking Letters. 2023;**5**(4):241-244. DOI: 10.1109/LNET.2023.3286443

[6] Iqbal W, Abbas H, Daneshmand M, Rauf B, Bangash YA. An In-depth analysis of IoT security requirements, challenges, and their countermeasures via software-defined security. IEEE Internet of Things Journal. 2020;**7**(10):10250-10276. DOI: 10.1109/JIOT.2020.2997651

[7] Zhang L, Yao Z, Zhang B, Li C. Scalable creditable-committee-based Blockchain consensus protocol for multihop wireless networks. IEEE Internet of Things Journal. 2024;**11**(18):29628-29642. DOI: 10.1109/JIOT.2024.3393927

[8] Chongqiang Y, Jian L, Xiubo C, Yuan T, Yanyan H. An efficient semi-quantum key distribution protocol and its security proof. IEEE Communications Letters. 2022;**26**(6):1226-1230. DOI: 10.1109/LCOMM.2022.3158906

[9] Cao J et al. A survey on security aspects for 3GPP 5G networks. IEEE Communications Surveys & Tutorials. 2020;**22**(1):170-195. DOI: 10.1109/COMST.2019.2951818

[10] Kim J, Astillo PV, Sharma V, Guizani N, You I. MoTH: Mobile terminal handover security protocol for HUB switching based on 5G and beyond (5GB) P2MP backhaul environment. IEEE Internet of Things Journal. 2022;**9**(16):14667-14684. DOI: 10.1109/JIOT.2021.3082277

Chapter 2

Current Challenges in IoT Security and Forensics: Strategies for a Secure Connected Future

Daniel R. Garcia Avila, Jerry F. Miller and Sundararaj S. Iyengar

Abstract

The exponential growth of the Internet of Things (IoT) has introduced considerable security and forensic challenges due to the rising complexity and heterogeneity of connected devices. As the adoption of the Internet of Things (IoT) continues to expand, so too do the vulnerabilities inherent to this technology, with threats ranging from the exploitation of individual devices to large-scale breaches of network security. It is imperative that IoT security frameworks undergo continuous evolution to address weaknesses in cryptography, authentication, and communication protocols. Concurrently, the field of IoT forensics encounters obstacles in the gathering and analysis of evidence due to the restricted memory and heterogeneous architectures of IoT devices. This chapter examines the critical aspects of IoT security, highlighting prevalent attacks, mitigation techniques, and the forensic methodologies employed to investigate compromised devices. Particular attention is given to the role of device heterogeneity, emerging forensic tools, and the impact of artificial intelligence on both security and forensic efforts. The discussion underscores the necessity for ongoing advancements to create a resilient IoT ecosystem capable of mitigating threats and enhancing forensic investigations.

Keywords: IoT security, IoT forensics, IoT attacks, IoT review, IoT security challenges, communication protocols

1. Introduction

1.1 What is IoT?

Modern life is defined by the pervasive interconnection between human beings and devices. Currently, nearly all tasks are performed with the aid of digital devices, facilitating the completion of tasks. This symbiotic relationship between humans and devices was made possible by the advent of the Internet. This technological advancement enabled the interconnection of computers (and people) on a global scale, paving the way for the creation of innovative and impactful applications that have transformed the way we live [1].

In the late 1990s, a new concept, the IoT, was proposed that further revolutionized this vast network of networks. The IoT is a network of devices (or "things") comprising sensors and actuators, software, and other technologies that facilitate interconnection and information exchange. The term "things" encompasses physical or virtual devices with unique identifiers that can connect to the Internet and communicate with each other. Some of these devices are equipped with embedded sensors to gather data from the environment, which enables the execution of deep analysis of data collected with a focus on the resolution of a wide range of existing problems [2].

A substantial number of solutions have been implemented since the advent of the IoT. These applications are ubiquitous across a multitude of existing industries, including health, education, transportation, and agriculture, among others. One of the most significant outcomes of this technology is the concept of smart cities, which aims to develop a range of IoT applications to address the primary challenges facing urban areas. Such applications include those pertaining to smart transportation, smart agriculture, smart homes, and so forth. These applications have one thing in common: the use of vast quantities of collected data for analysis with the goal of solving societal problems [3].

1.2 IoT system architecture

IoT systems are comprised of three principal layers: the perception layer, the network layer, and the application layer. The perception layer is responsible for interacting with the environment and collecting raw data, which is then transformed into digital signals. Sensors and actuators are located within this layer. Once data has been gathered, the network layer is responsible for ensuring communication between the various IoT infrastructure components. The objective of this layer is to transport the information gathered from the environment to the computers that are responsible for storing and analyzing it. The application layer represents the final step in the process, where all information is analyzed and presented to the end user.

This final layer is host to the plethora of applications that are being created nowadays in order to solve any problem [4]. As a consequence of the increasing complexity of IoT networks, it has become commonplace to encounter proposals for architectures comprising four to six layers. The rationale for this lies in the necessity to enhance the organization of the diverse processes occurring within these networks, with a particular emphasis on the role of cloud computing [3].

1.3 IoT application design

IoT applications present a variety of challenges during the design process, as numerous requirements must be met to ensure optimal functionality. These requirements are influenced by several factors, including transmission distances between devices, mobility, real-time communication capabilities, data transmission sizes, power consumption, and security concerns. Each of these factors plays a crucial role in determining the efficiency, reliability, and scalability of an IoT network or application [5].

Simplicity: Simplicity is a crucial aspect of the design of IoT systems. As IoT applications expand from a few devices to thousands, cost-efficiency becomes a major consideration. Reducing the complexity of IoT devices can help reduce costs and facilitate widespread adoption. However, simplicity must not compromise essential features such as security, performance, or battery life. Therefore, it is essential to strike a balance between simplicity and other system requirements to achieve cost-effective yet robust IoT applications. This trade-off is a central aspect of IoT design strategies.

Transmission distances between devices: IoT devices may be deployed in either proximity, within a range of 1 to 100 meters, or across longer distances, exceeding one kilometer. To guarantee effective communication across diverse environments, it is crucial to select suitable communication protocols. For example, short-range IoT applications may employ protocols such as Zigbee or Wireless Fidelity (Wi-Fi), whereas long-range solutions could benefit from Long Range Wide Area Networks (LoRaWAN) or Narrowband Internet of Things (NB-IoT). The selection of an appropriate communication protocol has a significant impact on the performance of the network, its power consumption, and its capacity to handle real-time communication.

Mobility capability: Some IoT applications involve mobile devices, such as vehicles in smart transportation or health-monitoring wearables. It is therefore essential that networks can maintain consistent communication despite the mobility of the devices. The additional complexity introduced by the handling of device mobility necessitates the implementation of more sophisticated processing capabilities, as the system must be capable of dynamic adjustments to changes in network topology. The selection of appropriate communication protocols, such as 5G or mobile mesh networks, can facilitate the optimization of performance in these scenarios.

Real-time communication: The necessity of real-time communication in IoT applications is increasing, particularly in contexts such as industrial automation and health monitoring, where immediate data exchange is crucial. The provision of timely responses is contingent upon the utilization of low-latency communication in these applications. Nevertheless, the attainment of real-time functionality frequently results in elevated energy consumption, as the necessity for frequent data transmissions is inherent. Therefore, a significant challenge exists in balancing the necessity for real-time communication with the conservation of battery power.

Variable transmission data sizes: IoT applications demonstrate a vast range of data transmission requirements, from small packets of sensor data to large video streams. For example, smart agriculture systems may transmit only a few bytes of data per packet, whereas surveillance systems may require the handling of substantial amounts of video data. This variability necessitates the use of diverse communication protocols that can accommodate both low and high data throughput without compromising performance.

Battery consumption: Battery life is a primary concern in the context of IoT applications, particularly in the case of devices that are deployed in remote or inaccessible locations. In such scenarios, the expectation is that the devices will operate for extended periods, sometimes up to a decade, without the need for battery replacement. It is of paramount importance to consider strategies such as energy harvesting, the implementation of low-power communication protocols, and the optimization of sleep modes when designing energy-efficient IoT systems. The implementation of an efficient battery management system has the potential to significantly prolong the operational lifespan of a device, thereby reducing maintenance costs and enhancing system reliability [6].

Security: Security is a fundamental requirement in IoT networks, given the sensitive nature of the data being transmitted and the potential for devices to be exploited in cyberattacks. IoT systems must incorporate a multilayered security structure to safeguard against unauthorized access and data breaches. However, the implementation of security measures frequently results in increased device complexity and power consumption, which is contrary to the simplicity and energy-efficiency objectives of IoT design. Consequently, the research community persists in investigating lightweight security solutions that reduce computational overhead while maintaining robust protection.

In summary, IoT applications and networks have a multitude of diverse and often conflicting requirements. It is of vital importance to achieve an optimal equilibrium between these factors to facilitate the successful implementation of IoT solutions. The ongoing development of innovative protocols and optimization techniques is intended to address these challenges, thereby facilitating the continued evolution of IoT technologies and their support for a diverse range of applications [7].

2. Understanding IoT security

2.1 General IoT security requirements

Ensuring the security of IoT systems necessitates the consideration of multiple dimensions, including the protection of data, devices, and network infrastructure. The principal objectives of IoT security are to safeguard information from unauthorized access, prevent data tampering, and guarantee the continued operational reliability of the systems. To achieve these goals, a set of fundamental security requirements—such as confidentiality, integrity, availability, and authentication—must be meticulously implemented to protect the IoT ecosystem against an ever-evolving array of threats.

Confidentiality. The objective is to ensure that data is accessible solely to its rightful owners, preventing any unauthorized individual from gaining access to the information. This is a fundamental aspect of ensuring the privacy of users' data.

Integrity. The integrity of data is maintained through the implementation of robust security protocols that ensure the accuracy and reliability of the information being transmitted. In any transmission, the data received must be identical to the original data sent by the transmitter, without any modifications. A variety of techniques, including hash validation and encryption, can be employed to achieve this objective. Such techniques can prevent the manipulation of data during transmission, which could have severe consequences.

Availability. The availability of data is a crucial aspect that must be ensured. This property is designed to guarantee that legitimate users can access their data at any given moment. This characteristic is a primary target for attackers who utilize denial-of-service attacks to obstruct user access to their data or disrupt application services [7].

Authentication. The process of verifying the identity of a user is referred to as authentication. A user's identity must be verified for him to gain access to their data. The purpose of authentication is to ascertain the veracity of a given user's claim to identity, thereby preventing malevolent attempts by attackers to gain illicit access that can be used to access or manipulate data from legitimate users.

Authorization. The authorization process determines the specific actions a user can perform within a given context. Once a user has been authenticated in a service, it is then necessary to ascertain which actions he is permitted to undertake, the operations he is entitled to execute, and the resources he is allowed to view, modify, or delete.

Non-repudiation and accountability. The concepts of non-repudiation and accountability play a significant role in the domains of security and forensics. In the context of Internet of Things (IoT) communications, the sender is required to utilize a digital signature, enabling the receiver to validate the transmission's authenticity and trace its origin. Furthermore, the generation of log records for IoT network operations is essential for maintaining a comprehensive audit trail, facilitating the verification of facts and the assessment of claims [8].

2.2 Vulnerabilities

It is becoming a common occurrence for attackers to succeed in exploiting IoT devices due to vulnerabilities that are both basic and easily avoidable. These vulnerabilities may include the presence of incorrect security configurations (or the absence of any security measures), unnecessary open ports, limited or weak encryption protocols, or a lack of timely security updates. Such issues fail to meet the minimum security standards that should be implemented in any digital device, thereby posing significant risks to users. The primary causes of these security gaps are the profit-driven priorities of IoT manufacturers, who often prioritize speed to market and cost-efficiency over security, as well as the absence of comprehensive legislation that addresses the specific security needs of IoT devices.

In their study [8], Siwakoti et al. examined the Common Vulnerabilities and Exposures (CVE) database to identify vulnerabilities in IoT devices, compiling a list of those with the most exposed security weaknesses. To gain further insight, they employed a custom query in the Shodan search engine to analyze the characteristics and services of these vulnerable devices. By combining this sampling strategy with insights from other research studies, they determined that the most vulnerable IoT devices include cameras, routers, smart TVs, Network Attached Storage (NAS) systems, Network Video Recorders (NVR), Digital Video Recorders (DVR), printers, smart meters, modems, and Voice over Internet Protocol (VoIP) phones.

In a comprehensive survey conducted by Neshenko et al. [7], the authors examined a vast array of academic literature and identified multiple critical vulnerabilities inherent to IoT systems. A significant challenge pertains to the physical security of IoT devices, many of which operate autonomously in unattended locations, rendering them vulnerable to malevolent interference. The authentication mechanisms employed are often simplistic due to design constraints, which leaves IoT communications vulnerable to spoofing. This can result in data breaches, impersonation attacks, and compromised data integrity.

Another area of concern is the use of encryption in IoT communications. Due to resource limitations, the deployment of robust encryption algorithms is often impractical, leaving communications vulnerable to decryption by attackers. Furthermore, patch management represents a significant vulnerability that is frequently overlooked. A significant number of IoT devices are deployed with factory-default firmware and are not updated when new versions become available. This issue arises due to a lack of user awareness and insufficient automation from manufacturers, who should implement automatic and mandatory firmware updates. Regular updates are crucial for mitigating a wide range of attacks by addressing known vulnerabilities.

2.3 Threats and attacks

The extensive array of vulnerabilities intrinsic to IoT devices provides malicious actors with a multitude of potential avenues for launching sophisticated cyberattacks. The exploitation of a single vulnerability in an IoT device can potentially compromise the security of the entire network, including components that are not themselves IoT devices. The most prevalent attacks targeting IoT systems encompass Denial of

Service (DoS), eavesdropping, Man-in-the-Middle (MiTM), and replay attacks [8]. Such attacks have a significant impact on user privacy, which has led to a growing sense of distrust in IoT systems among consumers.

In light of the considerable array of attack types, researchers have devised many frameworks for classifying these threats. In the studies by Siwakoti et al. [8], the classification of attacks is based on the specific layer of the IoT architecture that they target. This classification is structured according to the four-layer IoT architecture model, which groups attacks into the following categories: perception layer, network layer, data layer, and application layer attacks.

In [1], the authors propose a classification of IoT threats into four primary categories:

- *Access control attacks*: These encompass a range of malicious activities that aim to gain unauthorized access to a system or resource. These attacks concentrate on three essential security requirements for the IoT: authorization, confidentiality, and authentication. These attacks target the initial communication and registration processes of IoT devices within networks, where attackers can gain access to sensitive information such as device identifications, encryption keys, and signatures. Such information can then be exploited to impersonate legitimate users within the IoT network.

- *Impersonation attacks*: Impersonation attacks entail the manipulation of ongoing IoT communications through the use of false identities. One common attack in this category is node tampering, which involves the physical modification or replacement of an IoT device to gain unauthorized access to the network from the edge. Another noteworthy assault is the MiTM attack. In this attack, an assailant intercepts communication and impersonates one of the users, a tactic that has the potential to result in a data breach and significantly compromise privacy.

- *Eavesdropping attacks*: *Eavesdropping attacks* involve the surreptitious monitoring and analysis of communication channels. Tools such as Wireshark facilitate the examination of communications between users or entities, enabling the discovery of passwords, the acquisition of knowledge regarding communication protocols, and the evaluation of security features. With this information, attackers can perpetrate MiTM attacks, procure sensitive information, or gain unauthorized access to a network.

- *Denial of service (DoS) and routing attacks*: The objective of these attacks is to disrupt communication between legitimate customers and a specific service. Such attacks may be executed from a single node or a multitude of them, to continuously transmit packages to a defined service to overload the communication channels and prevent legitimate users from accessing the service. These attacks have a considerable impact on the operational costs associated with a given service. While denial-of-service attacks target the application layer, routing attacks aim to disrupt the network layer by modifying routing paths during communication, creating chaos within the network.

The existing literature demonstrates that researchers have employed a variety of approaches to classify attacks targeting Internet of Things (IoT) systems. These approaches include classification by architectural layers, vulnerability groups, and logical IoT processes. In their study [7], Neshenko et al. observed that single attacks frequently exploit multiple vulnerabilities within an IoT system. This observation leads to the conclusion that a more effective approach for improving IoT security would be to focus research on the attacks themselves, specifically analyzing their operational mechanisms and countermeasures.

2.4 General challenges in securing IoT devices and networks

The accelerated evolution and pervasive implementation of IoT technologies have given rise to substantial concerns about security, particularly given the prevalence of IoT applications that handle highly sensitive user data. The security of IoT systems presents a distinctive set of challenges, requiring a delicate balance between the need for simplicity and the implementation of robust security measures. The design of a universal security model is particularly challenging due to the heterogeneity of IoT devices, which vary in terms of hardware, software, and communication protocols.

Another challenge is the need to address vulnerabilities across the multiple layers of the IoT architecture. Each layer, from physical devices to cloud applications, has distinct characteristics and requires tailored security solutions, making comprehensive protection difficult to achieve. Additionally, the evolving nature of cyberattacks presents a constant threat to IoT security. Attackers are continually developing new techniques to compromise, control, or disrupt IoT services, further complicating efforts to maintain secure IoT environments [1].

3. IoT forensics

3.1 What is IoT forensics?

IoT Forensics is a subset of digital forensics and a growing field of research and discovery. The goal of IoT forensics is to investigate security breaches in the IoT system to understand what happened during a cyber-crime or security incident involving the IoT network, connected devices, storage systems, or cloud systems comprising the IoT network. By identifying and extracting digital information within the IoT system, security professionals can find the root cause of attacks or disruptions, immediately minimize the attacks, and develop control systems to counter similar attacks. The fundamental component in a forensic investigation is collecting evidence from the devices, logs, applications, and the IoT network, analyzing, and then preserving the evidence for potential criminal charges.

Digital forensics, particularly IoT forensics, is challenging due to the multiple types of IOT devices connected to the network and their varying operating systems and architectures. Due to the small size of many of the connected devices, onboard memory and processing power can be extremely limited, making it difficult to extract and analyze data before it is altered or deleted. Extracted evidence must be preserved intact, as close to the original information as possible, compounding the tasks of IoT forensic investigators and scientists.

Unlike other forensic investigations where evidence such as fingerprints and DNA can be directly attributed to a suspect, digital forensics occurs on the devices and networks in which they are operating, so the identification of the suspect can only be ascertained through circumstantial evidence. For example, if a suspect's computer was used in a crime, investigators would need to demonstrate that the suspect was at the keyboard (or near the device) when the crime was committed. Combined with IoT devices, connections, architectures, and the human element, an IoT forensics investigation can become very complex.

3.2 IoT architecture

IoT architecture is the framework that defines how the components of the Internet of Things interact with each other and how data flows through the multilayered structure. To handle the complexity of the IoT system, forensic scientists can approach an investigation by looking at the problem through the lens of the IoT component building blocks. The IoT architecture is commonly broken down into three to seven layers to identify specific activities. Although relatively well-defined, the IoT system is by its very nature an open, fluid system whose architecture lacks standardized protocols [9]. Variability of standards raises some interesting compatibility and security challenges, often leading to opportunities for malicious attacks.

As an initial framework for analyzing IoT forensic challenges, IoT forensic investigators use the expanded seven-layer architecture as a guide, exploring first the Perception (sensing/device) layer, the Transport (Data Transfer Protocol) Layer, Edge (Edge Computing) Layer, the Processing (Middleware) Layer, Application (Human Interface) Layer, Business Layer, and finally the Security (Equipment, Cloud, Connection) Layer [9, 10].

Perception layer: The perception layer is often identified as the sensing or device layer. This layer is comprised of multiple elements such as a variety of sensors, cameras, actuators, wearables, or other devices gathering data for performing some tasks [9]. Within this layer, any of the devices could become compromised and input false or nefarious information, viruses, worms, or malicious code into the IoT system. This layer is one of the most variable layers as it allows for multiple connections through dissimilar devices.

Transport layer: The transport layer uses specific protocols to move data from multiple connected devices to their destinations. This layer relies on IoT gateways to convert the incoming signals from analog to digital format. The gateways employ a wide array of data transfer protocols (DTPs) designed to transmit the data to on-premise storage or cloud data centers [9]. For the forensic investigator, the transmission of data through various protocols may conceal an intrusion or anomaly requiring a more detailed forensic examination.

The data transfer protocol is determined by factors such as the amount and type of data to be sent, the desired speed and transmission interval of the data, the anticipated reliability of network connections, the available power for consumption during data transmission, security requirements of the network and data, and additional communication requirements among the edge devices.

Various Data Transfer Protocols are used throughout the IoT network, each with advantages and disadvantages. DTPs such as Constrained Application Protocol (CoAP) and Data Distribution Service (DDS) are used extensively in industry and smart healthcare devices. Transport Layer Security (TLS) protocol is an important protocol used to secure communications between IoT devices across the network by encrypting the data. Simmons [Simmons seven-Layer] has identified some of the more widely used DTPs in the IoT transport layer system.

Ethernet for Control Automation Technology (EtherCAT): EtherCAT is an ethernet-based protocol used for industrial systems requiring real-time data updates. It is one of the most widely used IoT gateway protocols.

Controller Area Network (CAN) bus: CAN bus was initially designed for the automotive industry to enable different devices and sensors within a vehicle to communicate directly. This protocol has been adapted for a wide variety of other communication uses including maritime vessels, construction equipment, lighting control systems, as well as elevator and escalator controls.

Message Queue Telemetry Transport (MQTT): MQTT was designed as a lightweight protocol by International Business Machines (IBM) and is the most widely used protocol in the IoT system due to its "open-source nature and suitability" for sensors located in remote areas.

Advanced Message Queuing Protocol (AMQP) was developed by J.P. Morgan Chase for use in transmitting data within the financial services sector. A significant strength of AMQP is its built-in security framework that uses components such as Transport Layer Security (TLS) and Simple Authentication and Security Layer (SASL) protocols.

Edge layer: Due to the size of IoT systems with large numbers of devices connected through central hubs, slow transfer of data (latency) has become a significant performance challenge. To overcome this issue, scientists have developed systems and devices to process and analyze data as close to the source as possible. These are known as edge devices and form the edge layer of the IoT. Processed data can then be sent to other IoT nodes to further collect and process the data. "SMART" Edge devices can also include security features to detect anomalies and initiate damage control measures [9]. The edge layer presents several challenges through its pre-processing architecture which may filter out valuable IoT data before it can be processed or identified in a forensic examination.

Processing layer: The processing layer, often called the middleware layer, typically connects computers simultaneously (cloud computing) to compute, store, network, and secure data within the IoT system. This layer is the heart of the IoT system and is responsible for analyzing input data. Data is accumulated, identified, and assigned to appropriate storage within this layer. The data is aggregated from multiple sources and converted into a usable format for the Application Layer. In addition, data is analyzed using machine learning (ML) or deep learning algorithms designed to detect usable patterns within large data sets that might otherwise go undetected. This layer is an area of critical concern for the forensic scientist.

Application layer: The application layer compiles the processed data into summary information such as graphs and tables which can be easily understood by humans. Programs for device control and monitoring are elements of the application layer [9].

Business layer: Above the application layer is the business layer which employs specialized systems to further process and distill business insights, predict future trends, and drive operational decisions and important business functions based on the process data. Information derived from this layer is used by industry experts to improve efficiency, safety, and cost-effectiveness [9].

Security layer: The security layer provides software and protocols designed to protect and secure the equipment involved in the IoT system, provide cloud security, prevent data leaks, and provide secure conductivity for data transmission across the IoT subnetworks.

3.3 Threats and challenges in IoT forensics

Within the IoT architecture, security vulnerabilities top the list of IoT challenges. Security issues may arise in any of the layers and nodes that comprise the IoT system.

The lack of standardized IoT protocols provides a window of vulnerability to the entire IoT system.

IoT network devices are vulnerable to several network attacks, including Distributed Denial of Service (DDoS) attacks due to resource constraints (device power and memory capabilities), botnet attacks, and infusion of malware attacks. SonicWall reported more than 112.3 million malware attacks against IoT devices in 2022, representing 87% growth in cyberattacks over the previous year [11]. In 2024, the attacks continued to increase by more than 107% from a year earlier. More alarming is the 92% increase in TLS-encrypted transfers delivering malware across the network [12].

IoT threats will continue to increase, targeting vulnerabilities in third-party software and services that provide the connective tissue to the IoT. Traditional vulnerabilities have yet to be eliminated and remain a significant risk, especially for smaller businesses and organizations with limited resources for advanced security systems that are connected for their day-to-day lifeline to the IoT. These attacks are insidious, exploiting weaknesses in software updates, libraries, or interconnected systems, to gain access to sensitive data or systems. Unlike traditional, direct security attacks, these attacks are effective at bypassing standardized security systems as they gain access from inside the network [12].

3.4 Emerging tools and techniques in IoT forensics

AlShaer et al. identified several emerging IoT investigation models [13]. An investigation framework called the "machine-to-machine (M2M) framework" efficiently examines and analyzes a large amount of data with little impact on the performance of the IoT device. The framework effectively stores logs as evidence using Snort—an open-source, free, lightweight network intrusion detection system (NIDS) before conducting the analysis [14]. The M2M framework can be used for automatic detection of cyberattacks. Experimental results of the proposed framework outperform traditional machine learning techniques by achieving an accuracy of 88% [13, 14].

Another proposed framework is the Internet-of-Forensic (IoF) developed by Kumar et al. [15]. The IoF framework addresses the critical issue of IoT heterogeneity and lack of transparency of evidence processing by incorporating a blockchain-tailored IoT framework. Within a single framework, IoF provides a transparent view of the investigation process involving all stakeholders, including the wide variety of devices and cloud service providers. The framework has proven to be useful in maintaining chain-of-custody for evidence. Compared to other state-of-the-art frameworks, IoF is an efficient system that reduces complexity, time consumption, memory and CPU utilization, and energy consumption within the IoT system [15].

Investigative process models for IoT forensics: Researchers are developing more efficient and effective investigative process models for IoT forensics. One proposed investigative process is the Common Investigation Process Model (CIPM) for Internet of Things forensics. By identifying the 10 most common IoT forensic process models, researchers developed CIPM which combines 45 common investigative processes into four inclusive processes that include investigation preparation, collection, analysis, and final reporting processes. The system can be used to assist investigators in managing and organizing IoT investigation tasks [16].

3.5 Impact of device heterogeneity on IoT security and forensics

3.5.1 IoT devices heterogeneity

The IoT market is undergoing exponential growth, with an increasing number of companies engaged in the production of IoT devices and competing for market share. This expansion is particularly notable in the domain of smart homes, where technological advancements are being integrated into everyday life to enhance convenience and security. The implementation of smart home applications, such as smart locks and surveillance systems, has the potential to enhance the security of living environments. Furthermore, the incorporation of intelligent appliances and wireless sensors enables remote control capabilities, improving the overall comfort and convenience of daily life.

Despite the numerous advantages offered by IoT-enabled smart home systems, a significant challenge hinders users from fully realizing the potential of these technologies: the heterogeneity of IoT devices. The rapid development of increasingly capable and efficient IoT devices has introduced a significant interoperability issue within smart home ecosystems. Manufacturers often employ distinct communication protocols, security mechanisms, hardware designs, and firmware. In many cases, these devices are restricted to operating within proprietary networks, limiting interoperability and preventing seamless communication between devices produced by different manufacturers. Consequently, users are forced to manage multiple applications to control various devices, which substantially diminishes the overall quality of experience in smart home environments [17].

The heterogeneity of IoT devices represents a significant challenge to the process of IoT forensics, increasing the complexity of forensic investigations. The development of forensic software capable of analyzing any IoT device is a challenging endeavor, due to the diversity in manufacturers, firmware, communication protocols, and encryption methods. The heterogeneity factor is a crucial consideration in IoT forensics, and the development of standardized solutions could contribute to enhancing overall IoT security.

3.5.2 The matter protocol as a solution

The considerable interoperability challenge between IoT devices from disparate manufacturers has prompted the development of a communication standard to resolve this issue. The Matter protocol, developed by the Connectivity Standards Alliance (CSA), was designed to address the current challenges of device heterogeneity. It enables customers to manage all devices through a single application, regardless of the manufacturer, thus providing a solution to the issue of device heterogeneity. The protocol was developed to provide a unified solution to the management of heterogeneous devices.

Matter supports Thread for low-power mesh networking and Wi-Fi for high-bandwidth applications. The Thread protocol was selected due to its superiority over legacy communication protocols such as Zigbee and Z-Wave. These advantages include superior energy efficiency, greater scalability, and enhanced potential to resolve interoperability issues. Furthermore, Thread offers additional features such as advanced encryption, user authentication, multiple redundancy options, and the ability to support both device-to-device and device-to-cloud communication [17].

In their study [17], Zegeye et al. deployed a Matter protocol Testbed using development kits in a configuration that included open-source software tools, libraries, and applications. Their experimental results, demonstrated through ping tests, validated the interoperability capabilities of the Matter protocol. This represents a significant step toward achieving seamless communication between IoT devices from different manufacturers.

4. Emerging trends and future directions in IoT security and forensics

Artificial intelligence will remain a primary driver in the development of IoT security and future forensics. Integrating AI for more robust personalized authentication will continue to be a key driver for IoT security [10]. In the future, we anticipate extensive integration of distinctive individual behavioral patterns for authentication, such as analysis of keystrokes, and touch gestures including pressure variability on the device surface, voice recognition patterns, and other biometric data. The use of AI to expand biometric access will, however, be constrained by database size and availability for AI model training due to privacy and ethical considerations [10, 18].

In addition to access control for each device attached to the IoT, AI will be used to improve sensor technologies and their integration into the network. This will be extremely prevalent in the healthcare industry as more devices monitoring individual health using wearable devices are connected to the Internet. The use of these devices will continue to expose the IoT to potential security vulnerabilities [19]. Integration of IoT sensors in clothing and the connection of intelligent e-textiles will further expand vulnerabilities within the IoT system [18, 20].

4.1 Harnessing AI for IoT security

Artificial intelligence (AI) has become "de rigueur" in almost all aspects of our lives and IoT security is no exception. Researchers are incorporating elements of AI to develop harder-to-break cryptographic codes, secure communications protocols, and anomaly detection throughout the vast field of IoT forensics. One emerging area of great interest for IoT connectivity is AI-powered biometrics.

Biometrics—"… the set of technologies in which unique human physiological or behavioral traits" [18], are used for secure access, authentication, and verification of the individual user. Included in this group of usable human characteristics are fingerprints, facial features, voice, iris patterns, or DNA. Biometric traits provide extreme accuracy to verify an individual's identity [18, 21, 22] and can be used to generate hashes to securely store and process information locally on the IoT device [21, 23].

AI provides a new element in biometric authentication to improve its accuracy, reliability, and adaptability in the IoT [24]. However, challenges remain in incorporating biometric data into IoT devices. Awad et al. [18] identified challenges in the use of AI for the two most popular biometric modalities—fingerprints and facial recognition.

4.2 Potential solutions to address current and future challenges

Challenges abound in implementing effective IoT security. The sheer number of devices that are added daily contributes significantly to IoT vulnerabilities, as does the ad hoc nature of device connections which are in constant flux. Cisco estimates that more than 500 billion devices will be connected to the Internet by 2030, while Tech

Jury reports more than 127 new IoT devices connecting to the Internet every second [25]. The use of increasingly stronger authentication techniques competes directly with the limited processing power, memory, and energy constraints of the connecting devices, thereby limiting the improvements of onboard security systems.

As the world transitions to super high-speed data transmission and advanced network performance provided by sixth-generation (6G) wireless communication technology, the Internet of Things will be transformed through improvements in virtual reality (VR), extended reality (XR), video streaming and gaming, biomedical sensing and informatics, smart cities, artificial intelligence, underwater communications, autonomous underwater vehicles (AUV), and expanded autonomous robotics and cyber-physical systems, including vehicular ad hoc networks (VANETS) and flying ad hoc networks (FANETS), and adaptable underwater networks, as well as technologies that are just beginning to emerge from our research laboratories [26].

The metaverse will continue to expand with every type of commercial activity known to man. While extraordinarily great things will emerge on the backbone of the IoT system, things will go wrong and will need to be analyzed, assessed, and corrected. Vulnerabilities in the expanded systems will be exploited. Individuals and organizations will require greater knowledge of the systems in which they are operating, as well as effective risk assessment and risk management tools. Once a vulnerability has been exploited, impacts will need to be quickly assessed, corrective action initialized, and the vulnerability eliminated or mitigated.

As we look into the crystal ball of the future, these are a few of the areas in which we see the greatest IoT forensic challenges emerging.

Plurality and heterogeneity of devices: The plethora of IoT-connected devices will continue to provide security and forensic challenges. The sheer number of devices provides network and investigative complexity. Limited onboard memory and low sustainable device power further complicate investigations by limiting the time available for investigators to harvest evidence.

Standardization of the IoT: Combined with the plurality and heterogeneity of the devices on the IoT, the open software standards and protocols will continue to make it easy to connect but difficult to investigate. Attackers will continue to use encrypted data to launch malicious attacks, adding a further element of concern for forensic investigators.

AI in the IoT: Attackers will continue to use AI to proliferate innovative attack vectors in the IoT, remaining one step ahead of investigators and detection. Combined with cryptographic transport and third-party software, attackers will become more proficient in avoiding confrontation by obscuring their attacks from inside the IoT.

Chain of custody and collection of evidence: In the ever-shifting sands of the fast-paced IoT, evidence collection and chain of custody will continue to pose problems for forensic investigators. Due to low device memory, rapid edge processing, and further dissemination across the IoT, many local logs needed to provide evidence in forensic investigations are lost. Collecting and maintaining evidentiary data as close to the malicious or criminal activity timeline as possible will remain an IoT forensic challenge far into the future.

5. Conclusions

Although a relatively new area in digital forensics, Internet-of-Things forensics provides a rich ecosystem of study and investigation that will continue to grow far into the future. Estimates range from 32 billion [25] to more than 40 billion devices connected to the IoT by 2030. As the era of the 6G connection provides more opportunities for commercial activities and exchanges through the IoT, so too will at present opportunities for nefarious and criminal activities requiring skilled IoT forensic scientists and investigators. Through this chapter, we have endeavored to increase the knowledge base of IoT forensics, as well as inspire others to join us in providing a more secure IoT future.

This chapter identified the IoT concept by investigating the IoT system architecture and application design, and security as a fundamental requirement for IoT networks. The chapter also identified challenges and vulnerabilities in the IoT system and investigated common threats and attacks against the IoT. We identified current tools used in digital forensics on the IoT and looked at potential solutions to address future IoT forensic challenges.

As the IoT ecosystem continues to evolve, more research will need to be conducted to develop cutting-edge tools and techniques for maintaining IoT security. Better methodologies for IoT forensics must be investigated to conduct near real-time investigations and protect the evidentiary chain of custody. Scientists and investigators are making solid steps forward, however, the fluid, ad hoc nature of the IoT will provide many future opportunities for continuous research and investigation into the security of information and individual privacy.

Acknowledgements

Research for this chapter was sponsored by the U.S. Army Research Office and was accomplished under Grant Number W911NF-21-1-0264. The views and conclusions contained in this document are those of the authors and should not be interpreted as representing the official policies, either expressed or implied, of the Army Research Office or the U.S. Government. The U.S. Government is authorized to reproduce and distribute reprints for Government purposes notwithstanding any copyright notation herein.

Conflict of interest

The authors declare no conflict of interest.

Nomenclature

Zigbee	Communication protocol
Z-Wave	Communication protocol
CVE	The Common Vulnerabilities and Exposures database is a large list of publicly disclosed cybersecurity vulnerabilities
Shodan	It is a search engine specifically designed to find information about Internet-connected devices
Abbreviations	
IoT	internet of things
Wi-Fi	wireless fidelity
LoRaWAN	long range wide area networks

NB-IoT	narrowband internet of things
CSA	connectivity standards alliance
CVE	common vulnerabilities and exposures
DoS	denial of service
MiTM	man-in-the-middle
DTPs	data transfer protocols
CoAP	constrained application protocol
DDS	data distribution service
EtherCAT	ethernet for control automation technology
CAN	controller area network
MQTT	message queue telemetry transport
AMQP	advanced message queuing protocol
TLS	transport layer security
SASL	simple authentication and security layer
ML	machine learning
DDoS	distributed denial of service
M2M	machine-to-machine
NIDS	network intrusion detection system
IoF	internet-of-forensic
CIPM	common investigation process model
6G	sixth-generation
VR	virtual reality
XR	extended reality
AUV	autonomous underwater vehicles
VANETS	vehicular ad hoc networks
FANETS	flying ad hoc networks

Author details

Daniel R. Garcia Avila[1*†], Jerry F. Miller[2†] and Sundararaj S. Iyengar[1†]

1 Florida International University (FIU), Miami, Florida, USA

2 Florida Agricultural and Mechanical University (FAMU), Tallahassee, Florida, USA

*Address all correspondence to: danieltram3@gmail.com

† These authors contributed equally.

References

[1] Gugueoth V, Safavat S, Shetty S, Rawat D. A review of IoT security and privacy using decentralized blockchain techniques. Computer Science Review. 2023;**50**:100585. DOI: 10.1016/j.cosrev.2023.100585

[2] Uckelmann D, Harrison M, Michahelles F, editors. Architecting the Internet of Things. 1st ed. Berlin, Heidelberg: Springer; 2011. 353 p. DOI: 10.1007/9783642191572

[3] Wu C-K. Internet of Things Security: Architectures and Security Measures. 1st ed. Singapore: Springer; 2021. 245 p. DOI: 10.1007/9789811613722

[4] Chen K, Zhang S, Li Z, et al. Internet-of-things security and vulnerabilities: Taxonomy, challenges, and practice. Journal of Hardware and Systems Security. 2018;**2**:97-110. DOI: 10.1007/s41635-017-0029-7

[5] Alhamarneh RA, Singh MM. Strengthening internet of things security: Surveying physical unclonable functions for authentication, communication protocols, challenges, and applications. Applied Sciences-Basel. 2024;**14**(5):1700. DOI: 10.3390/app14051700

[6] Liu KZ, Yang M, Ling Z, Yan HY, et al. On manually reverse engineering communication protocols of Linux-based IoT systems. IEEE Internet of Things Journal. 2021;**8**(8):6815-6827. DOI: 10.1109/JIOT.2020.3036232

[7] Neshenko N, Bou-Harb E, Crichigno J, Kaddoum G, Ghani N. Demystifying IoT security: An exhaustive survey on IoT vulnerabilities and a first empirical look on internet-scale IoT exploitations. IEEE Communications Surveys and Tutorials. 2019;**21**(3):2702-2733. DOI: 10.1109/COMST.2019.2910750

[8] Siwakoti YR, Bhurtel M, Rawat DB, Oest A, Johnson RC. Advances in IoT security: Vulnerabilities, enabled criminal services, attacks, and countermeasures. IEEE Internet of Things Journal. 2023;**10**(13):11224-11239. DOI: 10.1109/JIOT.2023.3252594

[9] Simmons A. Internet of Things (IOT) Architecture: Layers Explained. Dgtl Infra [Internet]. 2023. Available from: https://dgtlinfra.com/internet-of-things-iot-architecture/ [Accessed: September 2, 2024]

[10] Zhang ZM, Ning HS, Farha F, Ding JG, Choo KKR. Artificial intelligence in physiological characteristics recognition for internet of things authentication. Digital Communications and Networks. 2024;**10**(3):740-755. DOI: 10.1016/j.dcan.2022.10.006

[11] SonicWall. 2022 Mid-Year Cyber Threat Report. SonicWall, Inc. [Internet]. 2022. Available from: https://www.sonicwall.com/resources/white-papers/2022-sonicwall-cyber-threat-report [Accessed: September 2, 2024]

[12] SonicWall, 2024 Mid-Year Cyber Threat Report. SonicWall, Inc. [Internet]. 2024. Available from: https://www.sonicwall.com/resources/white-papers/mid-year-2024-sonicwall-cyber-threat-report [Accessed: September 5, 2024]

[13] Al-Shaer M, AlShehhi K, Abdulla S. The internet of things (IoT) forensic investigation process: A state-of-the-art review. Challenges and Future

Directions. JISCR. 2023;**6**(2):150-161. DOI: 10.26735/DBEU2801

[14] Mazhar MS, Saleem Y, Almogren A, Arshad J, et al. Forensic analysis on internet of things (IoT) device using machine-to-machine (M2M) framework. Electronics. 2022;**11**(7):1126. DOI: 10.3390/electronics11071126

[15] Kumar G, Saha R, Lal C, Conti M. Internet-of-forensic (IoF): A blockchain based digital forensics framework for IoT applications. Future Generation Computer Systems-The International Journal of Escience. 2021;**120**:13-25. DOI: 10.1016/j.future.2021.02.016

[16] Saleh MA, Othman SH, Al-Dhaqm A, Al-Khasawneh MA. Common investigation process model for internet of things forensics. In: 2021 2nd International Conference on Smart Computing and Electronic Enterprise (ICSCEE), 15–17 June. Cameron Highlands, Malaysia; 2021. DOI: 10.1109/ICSCEE50312.2021.9498045

[17] Zegeye W, Jemal A, Kornegay K. Connected smart home over matter protocol. In: IEEE International Conference on Consumer Electronics (ICCE); 06–08 January. Las Vegas, NV, USA; 2023

[18] Awad AI, Babu A, Barka E, Shuaib K. AI-powered biometrics for internet of things security: A review and future vision. Journal of Information Security and Applications. 2024;**82**:103748. DOI: 10.1016/j.jisa.2024.103748

[19] Mariani MM, Perez-Vega R, Wirtz J. AI in marketing, consumer research and psychology: A systematic literature review and research agenda. Psychology & Marketing. 2022;**39**(4):755-776. DOI: 10.1002/mar.21619

[20] Fernández-Caramés TM, Fraga-Lamas P. Towards the internet-of-smart-clothing: A review on IoT wearables and garments for creating intelligent connected E-textiles. Electronics. 2018; **7**(12):405. DOI: 10.3390/electronics7120405

[21] Yang WC, Wang S, Zheng GL, Yang JC, Valli C. A privacy-preserving lightweight biometric system for internet of things security. IEEE Communications Magazine. 2019;**57**(3): 84-89. DOI: 10.1109/MCOM.2019.1800378

[22] Dass SC, Zhu YF, Jain AK. Validating a biometric authentication system: Sample size requirements. IEEE Transactions on Pattern Analysis and Machine Intelligence. 2006;**28**(12): 1902-1913. DOI: 10.1109/TPAMI.2006.255

[23] Hussain S, Chaudhry SA. Comments on "biometrics-based privacy-preserving user authentication scheme for cloud-based industrial internet of things deployment". IEEE Internet of Things Journal. 2019;**6**(6):10936-10940. DOI: 10.1109/JIOT.2019.2934947

[24] Oravec JA. AI, biometric analysis, and emerging cheating detection systems: The engineering of academic integrity? Education Policy Analysis Archives. 2022;**30**:175. DOI: 10.14507/epaa.30.5765

[25] Watters A. Top 30+ IoT Statistics and Facts you Should Know for 2023. CompTIA Community [Internet]. 2023. Available from: https://connect.comptia.org/blog/top-internet-of-things-stats-facts#:~:text=According%20to%20Cisco%2C%20500%20billion%20devices%20are%20expected,127%20new%20IoT%20devices%20connects%20to%20the%20internet [Accessed: September 1, 2024]

[26] Kaur B, Dadkhah S, Shoeleh F, Neto ECP, et al. Internet of things (IoT) security dataset evolution: Challenges and future directions. Internet of Things. 2023;**22**:100780. DOI: 10.1016/j.iot.2023.100780

Chapter 3

Post-Quantum Cryptography for Wireless Sensor Network Using Key Agreement Super Singular on Hyperelliptic Curve

Mohamad Al-Samhouri, Nuria Novas, Maher Abur-rous and Jose Antonio Gazquez

Abstract

The intersection of security and sustainability within wireless sensor networks (WSNs) underscores pivotal factors such as energy efficiency, resource optimization, energy waste reduction, and the sustained integrity of network infrastructure. This interplay ensures that deployments are not just efficient but also ecologically sound. WSNs comprise autonomously dispersed sensors linked to battery-powered devices, facilitating wireless data transmission. The optimization of WSNs through Fog and Edge Computing signifies a paradigm shift, diminishing reliance on central cloud servers. This adaptive strategy enhances WSN efficiency across diverse environmental conditions by streamlining data transmission to centralized cloud servers. In cryptographic systems, conventional approaches reliant on mathematical algorithms to secure communication channels encounter vulnerabilities. Quantum cryptography presents a more robust alternative to conventional methods, while post-quantum cryptography (PQC) employs algorithms resilient to both traditional and quantum threats. This chapter introduces a novel approach for mutual authentication and generating session keys in communications between WSN nodes. We use Super singular Hyperelliptic Curve Cryptography (HECC) with a small size by exchange key Diffie-Hellman (DH) to improve security in IoT and WSN. This method provides a promising mix of quantum resistance and integration into conventional approaches.

Keywords: wireless sensor network (WSN), authentication, Supersingular Hyperelliptic curve cryptography (HECC), post-quantum cryptography, public key infrastructure (PKI)

1. Introduction

The Wireless Sensor Networks (WSNs) associated with the Internet of Things (IoT) have enabled the development of comprehensive and sustainable solutions. WSN comprises independently dispersed sensors linked to compact, battery-powered embedded devices designed to monitor environments as predefined setups. These sensors gather data, facilitating wireless communication among nodes to relay transactions to a central point across the network.

The main aim of the IoT is to actively monitor and gather data on the physical environment, transmitting this information to a central base station. WSNs find applications across diverse sectors, from military activities to environmental surveillance and wildlife tracking, serving as integral components of smart cities, disaster management, energy, and healthcare [1–4]. WSNs provide timely and accurate information, essential for continuous monitoring operations. Their deployment in challenging environments demonstrates resilience to outdoor conditions, ensuring the availability of critical data even in extreme situations.

Moreover, WSNs provide real-time data, flexibility, and cooperation, yielding substantial advancements in numerous application domains. Their integration with IoT and big data has broadened their scope, with expectations that these technologies will assume an even more central role in our everyday routines, infiltrating aspects of our lives that were previously inconceivable just a few years ago. WSNs and sustainability are closely connected, affecting each other in various crucial ways. Energy efficiency plays a key role in this connection [5].

By incorporating efficient and lightweight cryptographic algorithms into WSNs, we not only address security issues but also reduce the energy consumption of sensor nodes. This has a dual impact on sustainability: it lowers the need for frequent battery replacements and extends the lifespan of devices, thereby bolstering sustainability efforts overall [6].

Another area where WSNs and sustainability intersect is in the efficient allocation of resources. Here, the security of WSNs benefits from the streamlined implementation of protocols between nodes, which not only enhances performance but also aligns with sustainability principles by minimizing resource wastage [7].

Moreover, efficient key management and regular updates play a role in curbing energy wastage, diminishing the likelihood of long-term compromises and mitigating the environmental repercussions of compromised keys [8].

To summarize, the integration of security and sustainability in WSNs addresses crucial elements such as energy efficiency, optimal resource utilization, minimization of energy wastage, and long-term network preservation [9].

This synergy is essential to ensure that WSN implementations are effective, environmentally friendly, and socially responsible. The progress of WSNs encounters significant challenges in sensor design, communication latencies, and security. These challenges impose noteworthy constraints in various areas such as data storage, processing capacity, power management, transmissions, and security. Data vulnerability arises when sensor networks face compromises.

We propose a novel security protocol that will be security is assessed through a formal analysis of ProverIf; the potential use of post-quantum cryptography (PQC) will be suggested as a solution to enhance key agreement protocol based on WSNs and IoT by Key Agreement Super Singular on Hyper Elliptic Curve [10]. In the following, we view contributions that are summarized as follows:

1. This paper proposes a three-factor authentication and Session Key agreement scheme based on HECC for WSNs and IoT.

2. Tracking evidence *via* Fog computing with catch Custody evidence *via* PQC into Blockchain

3. View proposed protocol is based on the HECC key agreement mechanism and introduces the challenge/response mechanism to establish authentication and key agreement mechanisms among Sensors and Fog computing and the Blockchain of WSNs and IoT.

4. The post-quantum resistance security of the scheme is guaranteed by the security characteristics, in the hyperelliptic curve discrete logarithm problem, and resistance into symmetric, asymmetric cryptography, and quantum resistance cryptography.

5. The proposed scheme is validated in several forms. The scheme's security is assessed through a formal analysis of ProverIf.

2. Layered architecture in wireless sensor networks (WSN)

In Wireless Sensor Networks (WSNs), data packets are transmitted to the Base Station (BS) through either single-hop or multiple-hop methods. In the single-hop method, a node directly transmits the packet it generates to the base station. Conversely, in the multi-hop method, source nodes route packets to the BS *via* a path that includes multiple nodes. Each node along the path relays the received packet (or, in the case of the source node, the generated packet) to another node until it reaches the BS.

WSNs encounter various challenges, including energy consumption, sensor node deployment, routing algorithms, energy efficiency, cluster head (CH) selection, and resilience. To address these challenges, researchers have developed multiple routing protocols and Medium Access Control (MAC) mechanisms. Additionally, optimization algorithms have been designed to determine the most effective route between transmitter and receiver nodes, aiming to conserve energy and extend the network's lifespan.

Two primary architectural frameworks prevail in wireless sensor networks: Layered Network Architecture and Clustered Architecture.

2.1 Layered network architecture in wireless sensor networks

In this architecture, numerous sensor nodes collaborate with a central base station, organized into five distinct layers as illustrated in **Figure 1**.

At the Application Layer, traffic management is handled, with a focus on ensuring data reliability through cryptographic techniques. The Transport Layer facilitates end-to-end communication, utilizing protocols such as TCP (Transmission Control Protocol) and UDP (User Datagram Protocol) to maintain data integrity.

The Network Layer is responsible for tasks such as routing, power conservation, memory management, and self-organization, which collectively enhance the overall reliability of the network. Meanwhile, the Data Link Layer ensures consistent data transfer by incorporating error detection, repair mechanisms, and efficient communication techniques, thus extending the network's lifespan.

Finally, the Physical Layer manages the transport of raw data, handling encoding and frequency management, with an emphasis on energy efficiency to support battery-powered sensor nodes. In **Table 1**, we present the layered network *via* protocol while using per-layer architecture.

In summary, protocol design in WSNs is a complex task that requires careful consideration of various factors such as application requirements, energy efficiency

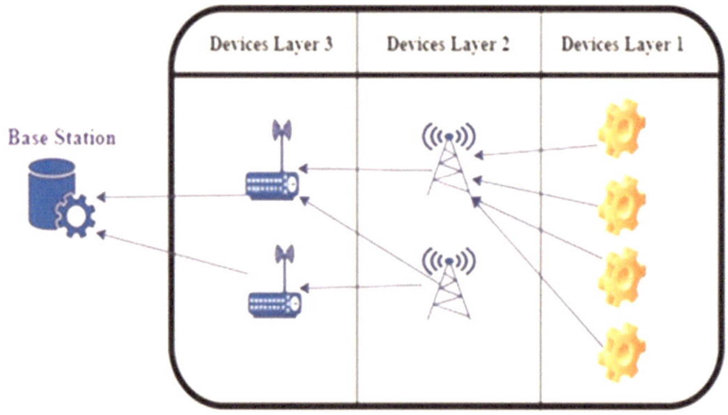

Figure 1.
Layered network architecture.

goals, environmental characteristics, reliability needs, security requirements, and communication constraints. Effective countermeasures must address these factors to ensure the reliable and efficient operation of the network.

2.2 Clustered architecture in wireless sensor networks

In a clustered design, sensor nodes are intentionally organized into clusters, which are often managed by a cluster head (CH). The CH serves as a coordinator and supervisor within each autonomously formed cluster. This architectural approach is intended to increase energy efficiency, network scalability, and data aggregation. Information gathered by each cluster member is combined at the cluster head, streamlining communication by delivering only condensed data from terminal nodes to the CH. Due to the autonomous and dispersed nature of sensor network structure, cluster formation and CH selection occur independently due to the autonomous and dispersed nature of sensor network structures (**Figure 2**).

Several protocols have been designed to operate within such clustered WSN environments. **Table 2** presents some widely used protocols associated with clustered WSN architectures [16].

These protocols address various aspects of clustering, including energy efficiency, load balancing, and communication optimization. Each protocol has its advantages and trade-offs, making them suitable for different WSN scenarios.

3. The advantages of fog and edge computing integrated in WSN

Fog and edge computing are pivotal in reshaping the landscape of WSNs by bringing computational operations and data storage closer to the data source. This strategic shift minimizes latency, enhances real-time processing capabilities, and introduces several advantages for WSN applications. These technologies empower local data analysis and processing, mitigating the necessity to transfer all data to a central cloud server.

Fog computing facilitates quicker decision-making by locally processing critical data, thereby improving overall responsiveness. Conversely, edge computing

Layer [reference]	Functions	Protocol	Countermeasures	Protocols depend on factors such as
Application layer [11–13]	Exchanging location-related data, synchronizing sensor nodes, moving sensor nodes, scheduling sensor nodes, querying node status, network security.	• CoAP (Constrained Application Protocol). • MQTT (Message Queuing Telemetry Transport). • Sensor Management Protocol (SMP). • Sensor Query and Data Dissemination Protocol (SQDDP). • Sensor Query and Tasking Language (SQTL).	• Use Spread-Spectrum or Frequency Hopping Communication. • Locating jamming and rerouting traffic. • Using prioritized transmission schemes to minimize collision. • Using tamper-proof locks or coating.	• Application requirements. • Energy efficiency goals. • Characteristics of the deployment environment.
Transport layer [13]	Reliable end-to-end data delivery.	• UDP (User Datagram Protocol). • Transmission Control Protocol (TCP) • DTLS (Datagram Transport Layer Security). • RPL (Routing Protocol for Low-Power and Lossy Networks). • 6LoWPAN (IPv6 over Low-Power Wireless Personal Area Networks). • AMQP (Advanced Message Queuing Protocol).	• Limiting the Number of Connections to prevent Flooding. • Authentication of every packet can prevent desynchronization.	• Need for reliability. • The conventional end-to-end retransmission-based error control and the window-based congestion control mechanisms used in the transport control protocol (TCP) cannot be used for sensor networks directly because they are not efficient in resource utilization.
Network layer [14]	Routing data sensed by source nodes to data sinks.	• LEACH (Low-Energy Adaptive Clustering Hierarchy). • AODV (Ad-hoc On-Demand Distance Vector).	• Encryption & Authentication. • Multipath Routing. • Identity Verification • Bidirectional link verification. • Authentication broadcast.	• Long-range wireless communication is costly in terms of both energy consumption and implementation complexity for sensor nodes. • Security mechanisms.

Layer [reference]	Functions	Protocol	Countermeasures	Protocols depend on factors such as
Data link layer [15]	Responsible for data stream multiplexing, data frame creation and detection, medium access, and error control to provide reliable point-to-point and point-to-multipoint transmissions.	• IEEE 802.15.4 MAC (Medium Access Control). • Zigbee. • 6LoWPAN (IPv6 over Low-Power Wireless Personal Area Networks). • TSCH (Time-Slotted Channel Hopping). • LoRawan (Long Range Wide Area Network). • Bluetooth Low Energy (BLE).	• Using TDMA and EC-Codes to minimize collision. • Using Random-Backoffs. • Using rate limiting in MAC admission control. • Using shorter frames to minimize unfairness. • Anti-replay protection and link layer authentication to mitigate exhaustion/ interrogation. • Jamming identification and and mitigating techniques.	• Manage access to the medium. • Error detection. • Reliable data transfer a trade-off should be optimized between the additional processing power and the corresponding encryption.
Physical layer [13–15]	Responsible for converting bit streams from the data link layer to signals suitable for transmission over the communication medium.	IEEE 802.15.4	• Use Spread-Spectrum or frequency Hopping Communication. • Locating jamming and re-routing traffic • Using prioritized transmission schemes to minimize a collision. • Using tamper-proof locks or coating.	• Energy Efficiency. • Range communication.

Table 1.
Layered network architecture.

involves direct data processing on sensor nodes, diminishing reliance on external resources. The integration of fog and edge computing into WSN significantly boosts network performance, scalability, and responsiveness, enabling

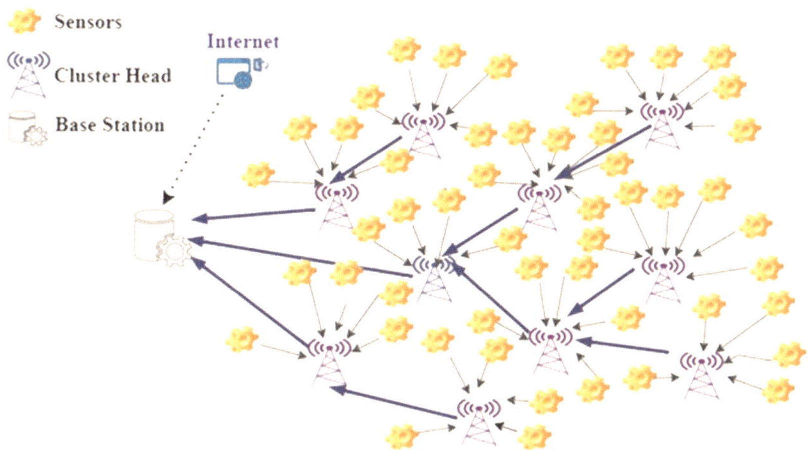

Figure 2.
Clustering architecture in a WSN.

Protocol	Descriptions
LEACH	A widely adopted clustering protocol employing randomized rotation of cluster heads to evenly distribute energy consumption among nodes [16].
HEED	An energy-efficient clustering protocol that uniformly distributes the energy load among sensor nodes using centralized and distributed mechanisms based on residual energy and communication costs [17].
PEGASIS	A data-centric protocol organizes nodes into a chain, where each node passes its data to the next node until reaching the sink, reducing energy usage by aggregating data and minimizing long-range communication needs [18].
TEEN	Designed for event-based WSNs, using a threshold-sensitive approach to detect and report events. Nodes remain in low-power mode until an event occurs, conserving energy [18].
SEP	Balances energy usage by selecting stable nodes as cluster heads in a clustering protocol [19].
TEP	Similar to TEEN, a threshold-based protocol for energy-efficient communication, dynamically adjusting threshold levels for event detection, reporting, and node activation [20].
MTE	Tailored for WSNs with mobile sinks, reducing the distance required to transfer data from CH to BS with threshold-sensitive methods for improved energy efficiency [21].
ESEP	An extension of the Single-Node Energy Model (SEP) that introduces three types of nodes: normal, intermediate, and advanced, with varying energy capacities [19].
CHIRON	Splits the sensing field into smaller areas, employing a Chain-Based Hierarchical Routing Protocol to create multiple shorter chains, effectively reducing data transmission delay, and redundant paths, and conserving node energy [22].
COSEN	Proposes a hierarchical chain-based protocol where one sensor is elected as a chain leader at each level or a level leader is chosen among all lower-level leaders based on certain measures in every round [23].

Table 2.
Protocol clustering.

Figure 3.
The advantages of edge and fog computing.

sophisticated and decentralized decision-making that adapts to diverse and evolving settings.

Let us explore the key advantages of edge and fog computing in **Figure 3**.

Features and advantages of edge computing:

- *Reduced latency*: Processing data closer to the source (sensor nodes) minimizes communication delays, leading to lower latency in data processing [24].
- *Improved scalability*: Distributing computation to individual sensor nodes facilitates better scalability, enabling the network to handle increased data loads more effectively [25].
- *Enhanced energy efficiency*: On-node processing minimizes the need for extensive data transmission, conserving energy in wireless sensor nodes with limited power resources [26].
- *Decentralized decision-making*: Enables autonomous decision-making on individual sensor nodes, reducing dependence on a centralized control system [27].
- *Increased reliability*: By distributing processing capabilities, the WSN becomes more resilient to node failures or network disruptions [28].
- *Optimized bandwidth*: Minimizes the need for transmitting large volumes of raw data, optimizing bandwidth usage in the WSN [29].

Features and advantages of fog computing:

- *Reduced latency*: Localized processing in the fog layer reduces the time taken for critical decisions, enhancing real-time responsiveness [24].

- *Improved scalability*: Adding computational resources at the network edge allows for a scalable and flexible infrastructure to support growing WSN requirements [25].
- *Enhanced energy efficiency*: Localized processing reduces the volume of data transmitted over the network, contributing to energy-efficient WSN operations [26].
- *Decentralized decision-making*: Localized processing allows for distributed decision-making in the fog layer, enhancing adaptability to dynamic environmental conditions [27].
- *Increased reliability*: The fog layer can act as a redundant processing layer, ensuring continued operation even if certain nodes experience issues [28].
- *Optimized bandwidth*: Local processing reduces the necessity to transmit every data point to a central server, further optimizing bandwidth [29].

In summary, the combination of edge and fog computing allows WSNs to dynamically adapt to changing conditions, making them well-suited for diverse and dynamic contexts. These technologies significantly improve performance, reduce latency, and enhance flexibility, enabling WSNs to effectively address the unique requirements of various applications.

4. Cryptography in wireless sensor networks

Given the vulnerability of sensor nodes to potential attacks and weaknesses, securing wireless communication in Wireless Sensor Networks (WSNs) is paramount. Tracking applications, for instance, are designed for specific purposes such as managing hazardous events that threaten human and animal safety. Consequently, it is critical to implement the necessary security measures to ensure uninterrupted operation of the nodes.

The effectiveness of cryptographic algorithms, when integrated into a robust key management system, is as crucial as the system itself. These algorithms must be precisely implemented for tasks such as data encryption, authentication, and digital signatures [30].

Selecting the appropriate cryptographic approach is essential for maintaining security in challenging communication scenarios in WSNs. The limitations of sensor nodes must be considered when establishing parameters between nodes. Factors such as code size, data size, processing time, and power consumption of cryptographic techniques must align with the constraints of sensor nodes.

Key agreement mechanisms emphasize the importance of prioritizing data cryptography. These protocols are necessary to ensure secure communication and data security within WSNs. Despite resource constraints, security services in WSNs aim to protect critical resources and information flow against attacks, even though the practicality of some schemes may be limited.

Establishing a secure infrastructure in WSNs hinges on key agreement protocols, which encompass various factors:

- Ensuring data confidentiality through encryption.
- Upholding data integrity using hash functions and digital signatures.

Processes	Key establishment of cryptography descriptions
Initialization	Setup of predefined cryptographic configurations: • *Key establishment:* Initialization of key parameters to enable mutual authentication between nodes. • *Pre-distribution of keys:* Preinstalling a predetermined set of keys on each sensor node. • *Public-key cryptography:* Asymmetric key pairs exchange public keys to generate a shared secret key without pre-distribution. • *Key agreement:* The techniques to establish a shared secret key without pre-distribution.
Random number	Secure key generation in WSNs relies on dependable generators to produce unpredictable keys.
Lightweight key	Secure communication between sensor nodes while minimizing computational and communication overhead.
Key updates	Mitigating long-term exposure risks and reducing the impact of compromised keys.
Distributed key	Using distributed key management techniques ensures the establishment of a consistent and secure key infrastructure.
Key revocation	Revoked keys must be invalidated, and a process for replacing affected nodes with fresh keys should be established.
Secure new nodes initialization	Secure bootstrapping procedure where new nodes obtain their initial keys from a trusted source or other nodes within the network.

Table 3.
The key establishment of cryptography in WSN.

- Authentication *via* digital certificates and public key infrastructure.
- Facilitating secure communication through encryption and authentication.
- Effective key management and maintenance of key freshness.
- Resilience to attacks.
- Energy efficiency in cryptographic algorithms.
- Implementation of security models.
- Intrusion detection mechanisms.
- Secure localization techniques.
- Adherence to standards like IEEE 802.15.4 and ZigBee security requirements.

Generating cryptographic keys in WSNs is a meticulous process designed to establish secure communication among sensor nodes. Due to the inherent resource limitations of these nodes, the key generation process must be both effective and tailored to their constrained computing capabilities. Here is a comprehensive outline of the key generation process for encryption in WSNs, as shown in **Table 3**.

4.1 Type of attacks in WSN

The generation of cryptographic keys in Wireless Sensor Networks involves a carefully orchestrated series of steps aimed at establishing secure communication among sensor nodes. Given the inherent limitations in the resources of sensor nodes, it is imperative that the key generation process be not only effective but also tailored to the constrained computing capabilities of these nodes.

Here is a detailed overview of the key generation process for encryption in WSNs [31, 32]:

1. *Initialization*: This marks the outset, where sensor nodes are initialized with a predetermined set of cryptographic settings. This involves the selection of encryption techniques, key lengths, and other parameters based on specific security requirements and the available resources.

    - *Key establishment*: This is a pivotal step where sensor nodes must mutually agree on a shared secret key for secure communication. Key parameter initializations play a crucial role in enabling mutual authentication between nodes. Methods for key establishment include:

    - *Pre-distribution of keys*: This entails presetting an established set of keys on each sensor node, making it suitable for WSNs with a constant structure.

    - *Public-key cryptography*: Leveraging asymmetric key pairs, nodes exchange public keys to create a shared secret key without pre-distribution. Computational burden may be a concern in resource-constrained environments.

    - *Key agreement protocols*: Techniques like Diffie-Hellman enable nodes to create a shared secret key without pre-distribution, calculating it without transmitting it over the network.

2. *Random number generation*: Vital for secure key generation in WSNs, sensor nodes depend on reliable generators to produce unpredictable keys. The randomness of the selected value is crucial for achieving uniform distribution and unpredictability.

3. *Efficiency key lightweight*: This is an essential consideration for establishing secure communication between sensor nodes while minimizing computational and communication overhead. Protocols are designed to provide efficient key establishment mechanisms suitable for resource constrained WSNs.

4. *Periodic key updates*: Regular updates to keys are implemented to guard against long-term exposure to potential threats and to minimize the impact of compromised keys.

5. *Distributed key management*: Given the dynamic nature of WSNs with nodes frequently joining or departing, employing distributed key management techniques ensures the establishment of a consistent and secure key infrastructure.

6. *Key revocation*: In the event of a compromised node or key, a key revocation mechanism becomes crucial. Revoked keys must be invalidated, and a process for replacing affected nodes with fresh keys should be devised.

7. *Secure initialization of new nodes*: When new nodes join the network, a secure initialization process is imperative to build trust and exchange cryptographic keys. This may involve a secure bootstrapping procedure, where the new node acquires its initial keys from a trustworthy source or other nodes within the network.

Wireless Sensor Networks (WSNs) are susceptible to a variety of attacks due to their inherent characteristics, such as wireless communication, distributed nature, resource limitations, and deployment in hostile environments [31]. **Table 4** outlines several common types of attacks targeting WSNs.

In summary, WSNs face diverse security threats that can significantly impact network performance and data integrity. Implementing robust countermeasures is essential to mitigate these attacks and ensure the secure and efficient operation of the network.

5. Quantum cryptography in the WSN

Quantum cryptography within Wireless Sensor Networks (WSNs) is an emerging field that combines principles from quantum mechanics with the need for secure communication among interconnected sensors. Traditional cryptographic systems, which rely on mathematical algorithms to safeguard communication channels, face increasing susceptibility as computational capabilities advance [39].

A notable technique in quantum cryptography for ensuring secure communication is Quantum Key Distribution (QKD). QKD enables the simultaneous secure generation of a unique secret key between communicating parties, which is then used for message encryption and decryption. The security of QKD is based on the principles of quantum physics, particularly the Heisenberg uncertainty principle, which imposes constraints on the precision of simultaneously measuring certain pairs of physical properties, with higher precision achievable when observing just one property.

Quantum cryptography ensures the confidentiality, integrity, and authenticity of data transmission within the network, offering the following fundamental features [40]:

1. *Quantum encryption*: Quantum states are used for data encryption, providing a robust defense against traditional cryptographic attacks. For example, the QKD protocol ensures secure key generation among sensor nodes, enabling authorized access to transmitted data. This protocol encrypts and decrypts information, maintaining data confidentiality.

2. *Quantum authentication*: Quantum authentication methods validate the identities of communicating parties, preventing identity theft or alterations during transactions. These methods use quantum properties to verify the source and integrity of transmitted data from initiation to conclusion. Quantum

Attack type	Definitions	The attacker it causes	How to do working	Processes to prevent this attack
DoS attack [31]	Flooding a network with an excessive packet, thereby impeding authorized users from accessing rightful services or resources.	• Node failure. • Network disruption or destruction. • Diminished network capability to provide service.	This attack acts as an aggregator, refusing to aggregate and hindering data transfer to higher levels.	• Authentication and Authorization. • Rate Limiting using Hash Function. • Identification Management.
Distributed Denial of Service (DDoS) attacks [33]	Using malware or exploiting security loopholes to hijack and control numerous machines and devices, launching a DDoS attack.	• Malware propagation. • Large-scale network congestion. • System overwhelms due to IP address inundation.	The attacker commands bots to target a system, overwhelming its IP address with requests.	• Monitoring the IP addresses of incoming data packets. • Traffic Analysis and Anomaly Detection.
Sybil attack [34]	A node replicates itself to create multiple copies, causing network confusion and potential collapse.	• Node duplicatio. • Disruption of fault-tolerant schemes like multipath routing, distributed storage, and topology maintenance.	A malicious actor creates multiple fake identities (Sybil nodes) to gain influence or disrupt network operation.	• Encryption and authentication techniques. • Unique Node Identifier. • Neighbor Verification.
Wormhole attack [35]	An attacker records packets at one network location, tunnels them to another location, and retransmits them into the network.	• Fake proximity of nodes. • Network congestion. • Increased packet retransmission, wasting energy.	The attacker tunnels packets between network locations and selectively retransmits bits, creating a false proximity scenario.	• Secure Time Synchronization. • Intrusion Detection. • Routing Protocols.
Blackhole attack [36]	A malicious node sends a deceptive RREP (Route Reply) message to the source node, claiming the shortest path, then drops the data packets.	• High packet loss. • Decreased network throughput. • Affects nodes far from base stations.	1. Source node broadcasts RREQ (Route Request) packets. 2. Adversary sends deceptive RREP with highest sequence number and least hop count.	• Secure Routing Protocols. • End-to-End Encryption. • Intrusion Detection.

Attack type	Definitions	The attacker it causes	How to do working	Processes to prevent this attack
			3. Source node selects path with the largest sequence number.	• Level Authentication
Traffic analysis attack [37]	Passive attacks deducing traffic patterns by analyzing eavesdropped information to identify strategic nodes for subsequent active attacks.	• Disablement of the base station. • Analysis of communication patterns.	• ID analysis attack. • Time correlation attack. • Rate-monitoring attack	• Hiding base station location. • Protection against rate-monitoring attack. • Data Encryption. • Secure Time Synchronization.
Eavesdropping [38]	Unauthorized interception and monitoring of sensor node communication by an adversary.	• Packet Sniffing. • Man-in-the-Middle (MitM). • Wiretapping: Physically accessing communication. • Remote Access Trojans (RATs): Attackers deploy malware for unauthorized access and remote monitoring. • Compromised Systems: Attackers compromise routers and switches. • Physical Surveillance: Eavesdropping on ATM PIN entry or keyboard login credentials.	The adversary will listen to messages transmitted by the nodes, or directly compromises those nodes. There are two eavesdropper attack. 1. *Passive eavesdropper:* The eavesdropper conceals her presence from the sensor nodes. 2. *Active eavesdropper:* The eavesdropper actively attempts to discern information by sending queries to sensors or aggregation points.	• Network Segmentation. • Key Management. • Authentication. • Encryption.

Table 4.
The type of attacks in WSN.

authentication systems provide strong resistance to impersonation and fraudulent attempts via Public Key Authentication [41].

3. *Quantum key distribution (QKD)*: A crucial component in quantum-secure communication protocols for WSNs, QKD facilitates the secure generation and distribution of cryptographic keys among sensor nodes while detecting eavesdropping attempts using quantum principles. Typically, QKD involves transferring quantum states, such as photons, between nodes, followed by conventional communication for key reconciliation and privacy amplification. WSNs implementing QKD establish communication paths that are demonstrably secure and resilient to both classical and quantum attacks [41, 42].

4. *Post-quantum cryptography (PQC)*: While quantum cryptography is reliable against quantum adversaries, it is essential to anticipate potential risks posed by future quantum technologies that may compromise traditional cryptography. Certain quantum-secure communication protocols for WSNs incorporate PQC approaches, designed to withstand attacks from both traditional and quantum adversaries. Techniques such as lattice-based cryptography and hash-based signatures enhance the security of quantum encryption and authentication methods [42].

5. *Efficiency and scalability*: Quantum-secure communication protocols for WSNs must be designed to operate efficiently within the resource-constrained context of WSNs. This involves minimizing communication overhead, energy consumption, and processing complexity to enable practical deployment. Scalability is equally important, given the widespread deployment of numerous sensor nodes in WSNs. Quantum-secure communication protocols should adapt to the growing number and complexity of WSNs while maintaining robust security standards.

Quantum cryptography and post-quantum cryptography represent distinct domains within the broader field of cryptography, each addressing unique challenges and operating on different theoretical foundations. **Table 5** outlines the key differences between these two areas [43, 44].

The BB84 protocol, named after its creators and the year of its publication, stands as the pioneering quantum key distribution (QKD) protocol. Introduced in 1984 by Charles Bennett and Gilles Brassard [45], B84 is the most extensively studied, analyzed, and implemented QKD protocol to date. Despite its prominence, various QKD protocols have emerged since its inception, with B92 [46] and SARG04 being notable variants leveraging quantum entanglement from BB84 and E91 [47]. While these QKD protocols are theoretically well-designed and structured, practical implementation reveals imperfections. Factors such as poorly constructed detectors, defective optical fibers, and general device imperfections within the QKD system introduce vulnerabilities to attacks. Uncovering and exploiting these system weaknesses constitute a fundamental area of research and study [44].

5.1 Protocol of quantum cryptography

The deployment of quantum cryptography introduces several challenges and drawbacks, notably the technical complexity requiring specialized hardware,

Features	Quantum cryptography	Post-quantum cryptography
Principles	Utilizes quantum mechanics to provide secure communication channels.	Develops cryptographic algorithms resistant to attacks from both classical and quantum computers.
Technique used	Quantum cryptography protocols, such as Quantum Key Distribution (QKD).	Algorithms designed to withstand attacks based on quantum algorithms, such as Shor's algorithm.
Target adversaries	Designed to provide security against eavesdropping attacks enabled by quantum computation.	Ensures security even in the presence of quantum computers.
Practical implementation	Widespread deployment is challenging due to factors such as cost, complexity, and limited range of quantum communication channels.	Many algorithms are efficient and practical, suitable for a wide range of applications, including internet communication, data storage, and digital signatures.
Scope of applications	Focused on securing communication channels between trusted parties, such as government communications, financial transactions, and critical infrastructure protection.	Broad applicability, can be integrated into existing cryptographic protocols and systems to protect against quantum attacks, including secure internet communication, data privacy, and secure authentication.

Table 5.
Summary of the main differences between quantum vs. post-quantum cryptography.

infrastructure, and expertise. There are constraints on the transmission distance of quantum information, and the technology demands significant complexity and substantial resources in terms of both technology and personnel. Managing the distribution of cryptographic keys presents challenges, and the system relies on dedicated quantum communication channels [44]. While quantum cryptography offers many benefits, it also has certain drawbacks, as outlined in **Table 6**.

5.2 Protocol of post-quantum cryptography

Post-quantum cryptography (PQC) encompasses cryptographic algorithms designed to resist the potential threats posed by quantum computers. Unlike traditional cryptographic methods such as RSA and ECC (Elliptic Curve Cryptography), which rely on the complexity of mathematical challenges like factoring large numbers or solving discrete logarithms for security, PQC focuses on developing algorithms that can withstand attacks from quantum computers.

The emergence of quantum computers poses a significant threat to classical cryptographic systems, as algorithms like Shor's algorithm can effectively factorize large numbers and solve discrete logarithms. Consequently, researchers are actively engaged in developing innovative cryptographic algorithms designed to ensure security even in the quantum computing era.

Post-quantum cryptography includes various approaches, such as lattice-based cryptography, code-based cryptography, hash-based cryptography, and others. These methods are founded on mathematical problems deemed challenging for both classical and quantum computers. The goal is to create encryption and digital signature schemes resilient against potential quantum attacks.

Given the uncertainty surrounding the timeline for the development of large-scale quantum computers, there is an increasing emphasis on standardizing and

Protocol name [reference]	Advantages	Disadvantages
BB84: Quantum key distribution: basic protocols and threats [45]	Unauthorized interception of the key is immediately detectable, ensuring confidentiality and integrity.	• Change in polarization. • Lack of digital signatures. • Predicament due to the source. • Need of a dedicated channel. • Distance and free space communication • Trojan Horse attack. • Tolerable error.
E91: Quantum key distribution [47]	Use of entanglement as a resource for secure communication.	• Not immune to all types of quantum attacks. • Dependence on trusted nodes introduces vulnerabilities and potential points of failure.
B92 [46]	Uses two states of polarization, providing an alternative to BB84.	• Requirement for a single-photon source. • Susceptibility to noise and channel loss.
SARG04 [48]	Highly robust against photon number splitting (PNS) attacks. The sender never announces its encryption bases, forcing a fraudulent receiver to store more photons to obtain reliable information.	• Quantum channel losses increase the Quantum Bit Error Rate (QBER).
Continuous-variable quantum key distribution (CV-QKD) [49]	Avoidance of the technologically challenging generation of squeezed light.	• Susceptibility to channel loss and noise. • Vulnerability to quantum attacks.
Measurement-device-independent quantum key distribution (MDI-QKD) [50]	Security is independent of the trustworthiness of measurement devices, relying instead on the fundamental principles of quantum mechanics and the correlations between entangled quantum particles to establish secure communication channels.	• Vulnerability to side-channel attacks. • Compromised devices can introduce errors or vulnerabilities.

Table 6.
Quantum key distribution protocols and their disadvantages.

implementing post-quantum cryptographic algorithms. This focus aims to ensure the long-term security of sensitive data and communication.

Post-quantum cryptography offers significant advantages, providing robust defense against both quantum and traditional cyber threats. This resilience ensures the long-term security of sensitive data and communications. Moreover, the adoption of post-quantum cryptography has spurred increased research, leading to advancements and innovations in cryptographic methods. This heightened focus contributes to the ongoing improvement and evolution of security measures in the constantly changing landscape of digital communication.

Despite its benefits, post-quantum cryptography also has specific drawbacks. **Table 7** summarizes the primary advantages and disadvantages.

Protocol name [reference]	Advantages	Disadvantages
Hash-based signatures, e.g., eXtended Merkle Signature Scheme (XMSS) [51]	• Practical Deployment by using cryptographic hash functions and Merkle trees. • Efficiency. • Conversion of a weak signature to a strong one with hash functions.	• Key Generation Overhead. • High Computational Cost. • Limited Signature Lifetime.
Lattice-based cryptograph, e.g., NTRUEncrypt, Kyber [52]	• Secure protocols and versatile applications. • Efficiency. • Simplicity and efficiency of algorithms applied to lattice-based protocols. • Growing interest among researchers.	• Large key and ciphertext sizes. • Complexity in implementation.
Code-based cryptography (McEliece) [53]	• Reliability and robustness from challenging coding theory problems like syndrome decoding (SN) and learning parity with noise (LPN).	• Large key and ciphertext sizes
Isogeny-based cryptography (e.g., SIKE) [54]	• Facilitates standardization and adoption, improving interoperability. • Exponential complexity of best classical and quantum attacks. • Active research in post-quantum cryptography.	• Performance Overhead. • Key Size and Parameter Selection.

Table 7.
Post-quantum key distribution protocols and their disadvantages.

5.3 Public key infrastructure (PKI) and post-quantum cryptography (PQC)

The latest encryption technology leverages digital keys and certificates to ensure information remains accessible only to its intended recipients. This comprehensive approach is known as Public Key Infrastructure (PKI), encompassing all components related to the creation and management of public key encryption, as illustrated in **Figure 4**.

PKI includes various elements such as software, hardware, rules, and procedures for initialization, key establishment (Public key, Private Key), Certificate Authority (CA), Registration Authority (RA), Public Key Algorithms, and the revocation or issuance of digital certificates.

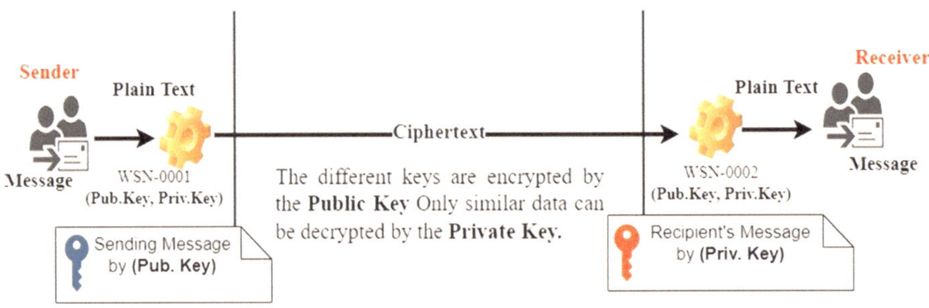

Figure 4.
PKIs for securing private key and public key message.

PKI is a widely adopted encryption method that establishes secure communication channels through digital certificates, thereby enhancing key exchange security between nodes. Although current PKI relies on cryptographic methods that are vulnerable to quantum attacks, the foundational principles of PKI remain relevant in the context of Post-Quantum Cryptography (PQC).

Post-quantum PKI involves using cryptographic algorithms considered secure against quantum attacks, necessitating the replacement of traditional public key algorithms with post-quantum alternatives. Some post-quantum cryptographic algorithms that may be used in a post-quantum PKI include:

Lattice-Based Cryptography: Utilizes hard mathematical problems in lattice structures, such as NTRUEncrypt and Kyber, to provide security against quantum attacks.

Hash-Based Signatures: Employ cryptographic hash functions to generate secure digital signatures, as seen in schemes like XMSS (eXtended Merkle Signature Scheme).

Code-Based Cryptography: Relies on error-correcting codes to secure communication, exemplified by the McEliece cryptosystem.

Isogeny-Based Cryptography: Leverages the mathematical properties of elliptic curve isogenies to construct secure cryptographic protocols, such as the SIKE (Supersingular Isogeny Key Encapsulation) protocol.

Post-quantum PKI aims to integrate these resilient algorithms into the existing PKI framework to maintain secure communication channels in a future where quantum computers are prevalent.

5.4 Our proposed protocol: Post quantum super singular key agreement by hyper elliptic curve cryptography

The principal aim of this study is to propose a protocol based on Supersingular Hyperelliptic Curve Cryptography (HECC) using a smaller key size compared with traditional public-key cryptography methods to improve security in IoT. The Diffie-Hellman (DH) key exchange is a notable technique for cryptographic key exchange, relying on Public and Private Keys to create a session key. These protocols allow two parties to establish a secret key through an unreliable communication channel, with authenticated Key Exchange (AKE) enabling parties to not only compute a common key but also ensure mutual authentication. This results in a verified session key, enhancing reliability.

The HECC protocol is characterized by progressive technologies poised to be widely utilized in the future. It provides a robust authentication mechanism based on small key sizes, ideal for lightweight security applications in digital cryptocurrency, web servers, microprocessors, e-commerce, and wireless communications [55]. ECC Cryptography offers many benefits compared with RSA and DH, such as reduced key sizes. However, HECC introduces further advanced solutions [56]:

1. Smaller key size with an equivalent level of security.

2. Bandwidth savings.

3. High connection speed.

4. Low power consumption.

5. Reduced computational cost.

Field	RSA and DH	EC-based	HEC-based
$F(2^{80})$	1024	160	50–80
$F(2^{112})$	2048	224	112
$F(2^{128})$	3072	256	128
$F(2^{192})$	7680	384	192
$F(2^{256})$	15,360	512	256

Table 8.
Comparison of key size encryption algorithms in bits to attain an equivalent level of security.

Consequently, HECC minimizes the key size needed for a certain security level, making it well-suited for secure communication in resource-limited wireless sensor networks, focusing on throughput, efficiency, and energy and as shown in the following **Table 8** [57].

Post-quantum cryptography utilizing supersingular elliptic curve isogenies presents numerous benefits, making it an attractive option for future secure cryptographic systems. We propose a post-quantum key exchange protocol called Quantum-resistant Supersingular Isogeny Key Exchange, based on supersingular elliptic curve isogenies [58].

Supersingular isogeny-based cryptography is designed to withstand quantum computer attacks, such as those using Shor's algorithm. Their compact key and ciphertext sizes are suitable for environments with limited bandwidth and storage capacities, enhancing network efficiency. Moreover, their integration into existing protocols and flexibility in adjusting security levels ensures compatibility and scalability. Ongoing research is expanding their applications beyond key exchange to areas like digital signatures, with efficient verification processes and long-term security assurances. Supersingular isogeny-based cryptography is well-supported by both academia and industry [59].

In summary, supersingular elliptic curve isogeny-based cryptography provides a promising mix of quantum resistance and integration ease, making it a strong candidate for safeguarding information in the impending quantum era. Its advantages in key and ciphertext sizes, bandwidth efficiency, and adaptability to various security requirements further bolster its appeal in both current and future cryptographic applications.

6. Proposed protocol

The proposed methodology consists of three main components: sensor nodes, fog nodes, and Blockchain. These elements are integrated to achieve lightweight authentication using a small key size through public ephemeral and private ephemeral keys by post-quantum supersingular cryptography. This methodology allows for the agreement on a joint secret key over an insecure channel between nodes using Hyperelliptic Curve Cryptography (HECC) and Diffie-Hellman (DH). The goal is to establish key agreements between nodes and create a secure session key (SK) shared among all nodes, based on lightweight transactions within WSN or IoT.

The protocol begins with initializing implicit certificates into random numbers and public key certification. Then, we present a security analysis for sensor nodes, fog nodes, and Blockchain, focusing on computational and communication overhead. Finally, the protocol is verified using ProVerif.

6.1 Registration phase

Implicit certificates are employed to reduce the storage requirements, making them particularly useful in resource-constrained environments. The proposed protocol is justified through performance, security, and comparative analysis. The calculation of the implicit certificate involves using both the certificate and signatures, as illustrated in **Figure 5**.

6.2 Key generation phase

In the key generation phase, the actual symmetric secret key (SK) is shared between the sensor (S), fog (F), and Blockchain (Bc) nodes. These nodes have established an integrated key agreement protocol, as shown in **Figure 6**. The sensor node (S) is identified by the identity ID_S key pair (P_S, d_S) for the public key and r_s for the private key, both of which are included from the setup phase. The fog node (F) is

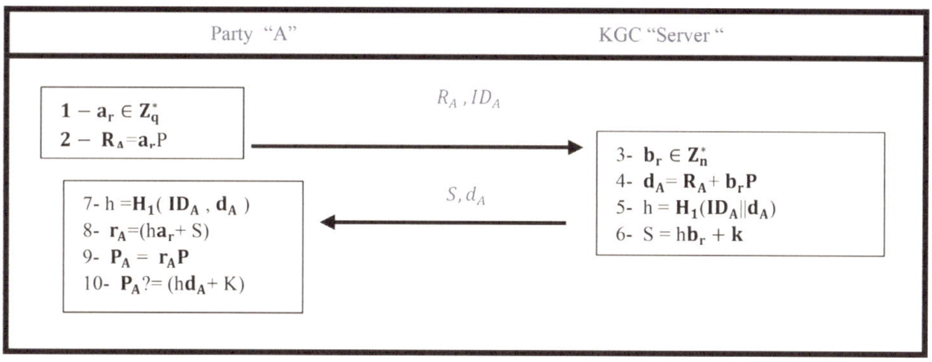

Figure 5.
The system implicit certificate protocol.

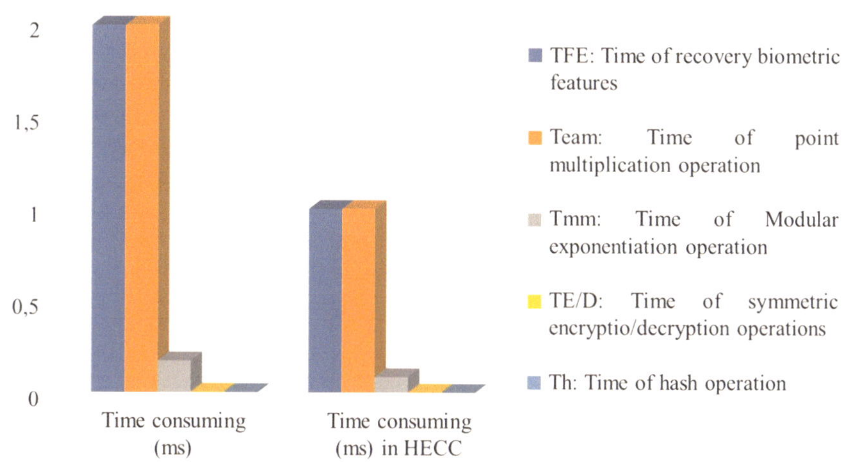

Figure 6.
The display of dashboarding of the notations, descriptions, and time-consuming required for computational time with HECC (ms).

Notation	Descriptions
p	Large prime number.
q	Prime (typically of 80 bits) up to (p − 1).
PA, QA, PB, QB, PC, QC	A devisor of large prime
ID_S, ID_F, ID_{Bc}	The Identity nodes are Sensor, Fog, and Blockchain.
Xs, Ys, Xf, Yf, XBc, YBc, d_A, R_A	The ephemeral public keys.
a_r, b_r, k	The Random Integer numbers.
r_s, r_f, r_{Bc}	The Static private keys.
ms,ns, mf,nf, mBc,nBc	The ephemeral Private keys.
(P_s, d_s), (P_f, d_f), (P_{Bc}, d_{Bc})	The public key with the implicit certificate.
K_{ij}	The Common keys between nodes are Sensor, Fog, and Blockchain.
C_1, C_2, C_3, C_4	Alias parameter.
A_1, A_2, A_3, A_4	The integrity between nodes with save hash 32-bit.
∂SF, ∂SBc, ∂FBc, ∂BcF, ∂BcS	The Formula of the Super Singular Protocol.
∅A,∅B, ∅Bc	The Isogeny key exchange.
SK	The derived session keys.
$Enc_{K_{ij}}$, $Dec_{K_{ij}}$	Encryption and decryption formula.
$H_1: \{0,1\}^* \to \mathbb{Z}_p^*$: Hash function	$H_2: \{0,1\}^* \to \{0,1\}\lambda$: Hash Function H_2. where the λ is security level.

Table 9.
Notation and description of our proposed protocol parameters.

identified by the identity ID_F key pair (P_F, d_F) for the public key and *rf*rf for the private key, included from the setup phase. The Blockchain node (Bc) is identified by the identity ID_{Bc} key pair (P_{Bc}, d_{Bc}) for the public key and r_{Bc} for the private key, included from the setup phase, as shown in **Table 9**.

In our proposed protocol, we have created authentication key agreements between three nodes that exhibit ACID properties (Atomicity, Consistency, Isolation, and Durability) using Diffie-Hellman post-quantum supersingular key exchange *via* public key infrastructure (PKI) in HECC. HECC features a smaller public key size compared to other asymmetrical encryption protocols. Given this, diversifying the set of possible post-quantum secure assumptions to build robust cryptographic primitives is prudent. We propose a post-quantum key exchange scheme based on supersingular hyperelliptic curve isogeny, known as the Quantum Resistant Supersingular Isogeny Key Exchange scheme, which utilizes HECC within the PKI framework [60].

6.3 Proposed protocol

Our proposed protocol (Post Quantum Super Singular Key Agreement by Hyper Elliptic Curve Cryptography) as shown in **Figure 7** consists of five stages that cover the novelty of our work.

The stages of our proposed protocol are as follows:

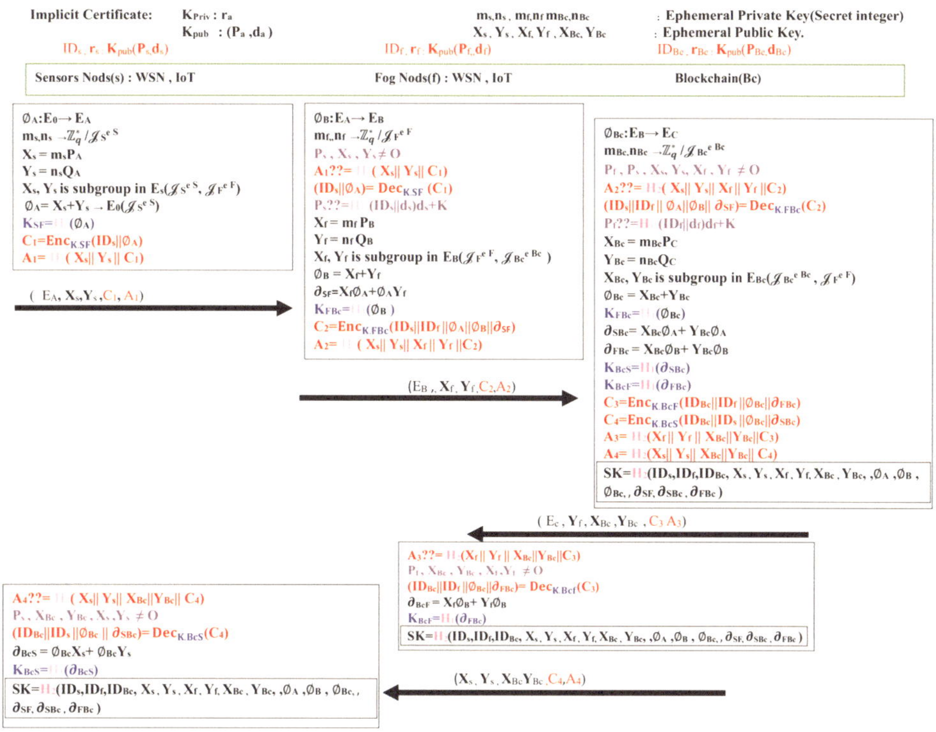

Figure 7.
Our proposed protocol (Post-Quantum Super Singular Key Agreement by Hyperelliptic Curve Cryptography).

1. *Sensor device initialization:* The **Sensor Node(S)** senses transactions by selecting secret random numbers by ephemeral private key into sensor transactions $\mathbf{m_S}$, $\mathbf{n_S}$, then computes the public key by HECC into Points $X_s = m_s\mathbf{P_A}$ and $Y_s = n_s\mathbf{Q_A}$, which is P and Q is The Point of the Elliptic curve. Next, it calculates common key K_{SF}=$H_1(\varnothing_A)$ by Using a Random number of sensor transactions, then calculates the Isogeny key by $\varnothing_A = X_s + Y_s$ for sensors nodes. Therefore, it derive Encryption identity and Isogeny (ID_S, $\varnothing_A$) by Alias parameter C_1=$Enc_{K.SF}$ $(ID_s||\varnothing_A)$. In The last transactions in the sensor's nodes, the Initialization Device creates integrity between nodes with hash functions $A_1 = H_2(X_s|| Y_s || C_1)$ using Alias name A_1. Then, the batch transaction to the Fog node as $M_1 = (E_A, X_s, Y_s, C_1, A_1)$ is submitted.

2. *Upon receiving message into fog node (F)*: In The **Fog Node(F) Upon** receiving from Sensors M1 = $(E_A, X_s, Y_s, C_1, A_1)$, check the integrity of the $A_1?? = H_2(X_s|| Y_s|| C_1)$ in fog node, IF authenticated, the transaction is admitted Else that abort communications. Therefore, decrypt (ID_S) by function $Dec_{K.SF}$ (C_1) and verify public key $\mathbf{P_S}? = \mathbf{H_1}(\mathbf{ID_S}\|\ \mathbf{d_S})\mathbf{d_S} + \mathbf{K}$, IF authenticated, check $\mathbf{P_S}, \mathbf{X_S}, \mathbf{Ys} \neq \mathbf{O}$ with not equal infinity **Else** abort communication. Into fog computing selects a secret random number by ephemeral private key into the sensor transactions $\mathbf{m_f}$, $\mathbf{n_f}$, Then computes the public key by HECC into Points $X_f = m_f\mathbf{P_B}$ and $Y_f = n_f\mathbf{Q_B}$ which is P_B and Q_B is The Point of the Elliptic curve. Then calculate the Isogeny key by $\varnothing_B = X_f + Y_f$ for sensor nodes. Therefore, calculate the

supersingular point of the ECC by $\partial_{SF} = X_f\varnothing_A + Y_f\varnothing_A$; next, compute common key $K_{FBc} = H_1(\ _B)$. Then, derive the Encryption identity parameter of $(ID_s||\ ID_f\ ||\varnothing_A||\varnothing_B||\ \partial_{SF})$ by Alias parameter $C_2=Enc_{K.FBc}\ (ID_s||\ ID_f\ ||\varnothing_A||\varnothing_B||\ \partial_{SF})$. In The last transactions in the Fog nodes in the middle Device, create integrity between nodes with hash functions $A_2 = H_2(X_s||\ Y_s||\ X_f\ ||\ Y_f\ ||C_2)$ using the alias name A_2. Then, submit the batch transaction to the Blockchain node as $M_2 = (E_B, \mathbf{X_f}, \mathbf{Y_f}, C_2, A_2)$.

3. *Upon receiving message to blockchain node(Bc)*: Upon receiving $M_2 = (E_B, \mathbf{X_f}, \mathbf{Y_f}, C_2, A_2)$, checked $A_2?? = H_2(X_s||\ Y_s||\ X_f\ ||\ Y_f\ ||C_2)$ with Blockchain node; if a match, the process is admitting in the Blockchain with a parameter. Else, that rejects and aborts transactions because the parameter is a mismatch parameter. Therefore, decrypt the parameter into Blockchain node $(ID_s||\ ID_f\ ||\varnothing_A||\varnothing_B||\ \partial_{SF})$ by using the function $Dec_{K.FBc}(C_2)$ and verify the public key in the Blockchain $\mathbf{P_F}? = \mathbf{H_1}(\ \mathbf{ID_F}||\ \mathbf{d_F})\mathbf{d_F} + \mathbf{K}$, If a match, check $P_f, P_s, X_s, Y_s, X_f, Y_f \neq O$ with not equal infinity; else, abort communication.

Consequently, for every transaction in the Blockchain, select a secret random number by ephemeral private key into the Blockchain $\mathbf{m_{Bc}}, \mathbf{n_{Bc}}$. By using ephemeral public key $X_{Bc} = m_{Bc}\mathbf{P_c}$ and $Y_{Bc} = n_{Bc}\mathbf{Q_c}$, which is P and Q is The Point of the elliptic curve. Then, calculate the Isogeny key by ephemeral Public Key point of the blockchain $\varnothing_{Bc} = X_{Bc} + Y_{Bc}$ for Blockchain. Next, compute common key $K_{FBc} = H_1(\varnothing_{Bc})$; therefore, calculate the point of the supersingular into blockchain for sensor devices $\partial_{SBc} = X_{Bc}\varnothing_A + Y_{Bc}\varnothing_A$ and fog computing $\partial_{FBc} = X_{Bc}\varnothing_B + Y_{Bc}\varnothing_{(E)}$.

Then, compute the common key for sensors and Blockchain $K_{BcS}=H_1(\partial_{SBc})$ and compute the common key for fog and Blockchain $K_{BcF}=H_1(\partial_{FBc})$; then, compute encryption by fog and Blockchain $C_3=Enc_{K.BcF}\ (ID_{Bc}||\ ID_f\ ||\varnothing_{Bc}||\ \partial_{FBc})$ by Alias parameter C_3, and compute encryption by sensors and Blockchain $C_4=Enc_{K.BcS}\ (ID_{Bc}||\ ID_s\ ||\varnothing_{Bc}||\ \partial_{SBc})$ by Alias parameter C_4. Then, create integrity between Blockchain and fog computing by using hash functions $A_3 = H_2(X_f\ ||\ Y_f||\ X_{Bc}||\ Y_{Bc}||\ C_3)$ with using Alias name A_3 and create integrity between Blockchain and sensors with using hash functions $A_4 = H_2(X_s||\ Y_s||\ X_{Bc}||\ Y_{Bc}||\ C_4)$ with using Alias name A_4.

At the last transactions in the Blockchain, create a session key between the Sensors, fog computing, and Blockchain by using identity devices and public key and supersingular formula at $SK=H_2(\mathbf{ID_s}, \mathbf{ID_f}, \mathbf{ID_{Bc}}, \mathbf{X_s}, \mathbf{Y_s}, \mathbf{X_f}, \mathbf{Y_f}, \mathbf{X_{Bc}}, \mathbf{Y_{Bc}}, \boldsymbol{\varnothing_A}, \boldsymbol{\varnothing_B}, \boldsymbol{\varnothing_{Bc}}, \boldsymbol{\partial_{SF}}, \boldsymbol{\partial_{SBc}}, \boldsymbol{\partial_{FBc}})$ in the Blockchain node. Therefore, send the message $M_3 = (E_c, \mathbf{Y_f}, \mathbf{X_{Bc}}, \mathbf{Y_{Bc}}, C_3, A_3)$ is sent backward to the fog node.

4. *Backward message from blockchain to fog:* Upon receiving of $M_3 = (E_c, \mathbf{Y_f}, \mathbf{X_{Bc}}, \mathbf{Y_{Bc}}, C_3, A_3)$ to fog computing, verify message into fog by $A_3?? = H_2(X_f\ ||\ Y_f\ ||\ X_{Bc}||\ Y_{Bc}||C_3)$. If a match, check $\mathbf{P_f}, \mathbf{X_{Bc}}, \mathbf{Y_{Bc}}, \mathbf{X_f}, \mathbf{Y_f} \neq \mathbf{O}$ with constraint, not equal infinity; else, abort communication. Then, decrypt into Blockchain and fog by $(ID_{Bc}||\ ID_f\ ||\varnothing_{Bc}||\ \partial_{FBc})$ by function $Dec_{SF}(C_3)$. Hence, calculate the point of the supersingular into Blockchain for fog devices into backward $\partial_{BcF} = X_f\varnothing_B + Y_f\varnothing_B$. Next, compute the common key between Blockchain and fog computing $K_{BcF}=H_1(\partial_{BcF})$.

5. At the last transactions, create a session key between sensors and fog computing and Blockchain $SK=H_2(ID_s, ID_f, ID_{Bc}, X_s, Y_s, X_f, Y_f, X_{Bc}, Y_{Bc}, \varnothing_A, \varnothing_B, \varnothing_{Bc}, \partial_{SF}, \partial_{SBc}, \partial_{FBc})$ into fog computing, Therefore, the message $M_4 = (\mathbf{X_s}, \mathbf{Y_s}, \mathbf{X_{Bc}}, \mathbf{Y_{Bc}}, C_4, A_4)$ is sent backward to the sensor's Node.

6. *Sensor device termination:* Upon receiving of $\mathbf{M_4} = (\mathbf{X_s}, \mathbf{Y_s}, \mathbf{X_{Bc}}, \mathbf{Y_{Bc}}, C_4, A_4)$ to sensor nodes, verify message into sensors by $A_4?? = H_2(X_s \| Y_s \| X_{Bc} \| Y_{Bc} \| C_4)$. If a match, check $\mathbf{P_s}, \mathbf{X_{Bc}}, \mathbf{Y_{Bc}}, \mathbf{X_s}, \mathbf{Y_s} \neq \mathbf{O}$ with constraint not equal infinity; else, abort communication. Then, decrypt into blockchain and sensors devices by $(ID_{Bc} \| ID_S \| \varnothing_{Bc} \| \partial_{SBc})$ by function $Dec_{KBcS}(C_4)$. Hence, calculate the point of the super singular into Blockchain for fog devices into backward $\partial_{BcS} = \varnothing_{Bc} X_s + \varnothing_{Bc} Y_s$. Next, compute the common key between Blockchain and fog computing $K_{BcS} = H_1(\partial_{BcS})$.

7. At the last transactions, create a session key between sensors and fog computing and Blockchain $SK=H_2(\mathbf{ID_s}, \mathbf{ID_f}, \mathbf{ID_{Bc}}, \mathbf{X_s}, \mathbf{Y_s}, \mathbf{X_f}, \mathbf{Y_f}, \mathbf{X_{Bc}}, \mathbf{Y_{Bc}}, \boldsymbol{\varnothing_A}, \boldsymbol{\varnothing_B}, \boldsymbol{\varnothing_{Bc}}, \boldsymbol{\partial_{SF}}, \boldsymbol{\partial_{SBc}}, \boldsymbol{\partial_{FBc}})$ into Sensor Devices.

7. Security analysis

This protocol provides a secure encrypted channel over an insecure network. It ensures authentication by key agreement among three nodes through encryption, decryption, and integrity security. Below, we present the security analysis of our proposed protocol by comparing it with related works using the same benchmark, as shown in **Tables 10** and **11**. These tables display the HECC's time consumption (in milliseconds) and bit length for each transaction.

Then, we analyze the performance of the scheme in analyzed from two aspects computation overhead and communication in overhead, and the scheme is proven to be suitable for resource constrained WSNs through comparisons with other schemes.

7.1 Computational overhead

The computational overhead is mainly point multiplication, modular exponentiation, symmetric encryption/decryption, hashing, and so forth. The computational overhead of || and concatenation is very small and negligible compared

Notations	Descriptions	Time-consuming (ms)	Time-consuming (ms) in HECC
T_{FE}	Time of recovery biometric features.	1.989	0.9945
T_{eam}	Time of point multiplication operation.	1.989	0.9945
T_{mm}	Time of modular exponentiation operation.	0.171	0.085
$T_{E/D}$	Time of symmetric encryption/decryption operations.	0.00325	0.0016
T_h	Time of hash operation.	0.0026	0.0013

Table 10.
The notations, descriptions, and time-consuming required for computational time with HECC.

Notation	Description	Length (bit)	Length HECC (bit)
L_{ID}	Identity length	32	32
L_h	Hash value length	160	32
L_{FE}	Fuzzy extractor public data length	128	128
L_r	Random number length	128	128
L_T	Timestamp length	32	32
L_{ECC}	Points of an elliptic curve (public key) length	160	80
$L_{E/D}$	Symmetric encryption/decryption data length	128	128

Table 11.
The notations, descriptions, and lengths required for communication data with HECC.

to other operations. From the computational time consumption in **Table 10** and **Figure 6**, we can see the notations for point multiplication T_{eam} symmetric encryption/decryption $T_{E/D}$ and hash operation T_h; the value of **Table 10** is represented from an article (authentication and key agreement scheme for wireless sensor networks) [61].

The comparison of computational and time computational (ms) overheads for each node is shown in **Tables 12** and **13**; the **Figure 8** displays the computational overhead (ms).

This scheme uses the HECC-based key agreement scheme, and the point multiplication operation overhead is higher than that of other schemes. To have supersingular point multiplication *via* PQC. The hash function is lightweight compared with related work except for reference [65].

7.2 Communication overhead

The communication overhead is mainly for the data lengths of identity hash value, random numbers, points of elliptic curve (public key), and symmetric encryption/decryption data. **Table 14** displays the comparison of communication overheads of related work based on **Table 11** via the length of bits for HECC. The values from **Table 10** have been used [61].

Reference	First node	Second node	Third node	Time computational overhead
[62]	$13Th + 1T_{FE}$	$18Th$	$6Th$	$37Th + 1T_{FE}$
[63]	$2T_{ecm} + 12Th + 1\, T_{FE}$	$10Th + 1\, T_{E/D}$	$2T_{ecm} + 5Th + 1\, T_{E/D}$	$4T_{ecm} + 27Th + 2\, T_{FE} + 1\, T_{E/D}$
[64]	$2T_{ecm} + 14Th + 1T_{FE}$	$13Th$	$2T_{ecm} + 7Th$	$4T_{ecm} + 34Th + 1\, T_{FE}$
[65]	$4T_{ecm} + 8Th + T_{E/D}$	$2T_{ecm} + 5Th + T_{E/D}$	$2T_{ecm} + 2Th$	$8T_{ecm} + 15Th + 2\, T_{E/D}$
[61]	$5T_{ecm} + 22Th + 1T_{FE}$	$4Tecm + 18Th$	$3T_{ecm} + 8Th$	$12T_{ecm} + 48Th + 1T_{FE}$
Our proposed	$6T_{ecm} + 5Th + 2T_{E/D}$	$10T_{ecm} + 6Th + 3T_{E/D}$	$8T_{ecm} + 6Th + 3\, T_{E/D}$	$24T_{ecm} + 18Th + 8T_{E/D}$

Table 12.
Comparison of computational overhead.

Reference	First node	Second node	Third node	Time computational overhead (ms)
[62]	2.0228	0.0468	0.0156	2.0852
[63]	5.9982	0.029	3.994	10.02
[64]	6.0034	0.0338	3.9962	10.033
[65]	7.98005	3.99425	4.0092	15.957
[61]	11.9912	8.0228	7.9768	25.9818
Our proposed	5.9802	9.9604	7.9724	23.913

Table 13.
Comparison of time computational overhead (ms).

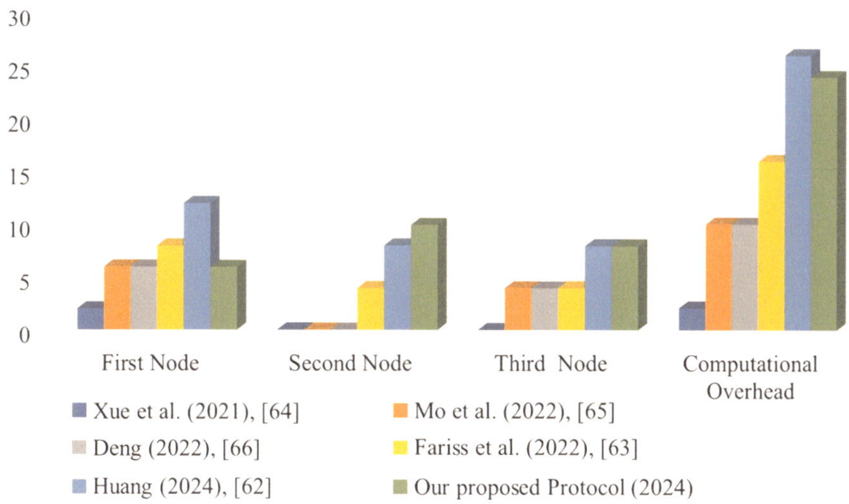

Figure 8.
The display of dashboarding of computational overhead (ms).

Table 15 and **Figure 9** show the comparison of communication overheads in bits with our proposed protocol (Post-Quantum Super Singular Key Agreement by Hyper Elliptic Curve Cryptography).

7.3 Informal analysis

This scheme can resist many common attacks and effectively address the short-comings of existing schemes. We introduced an informal security evaluation of the proposed protocol in this section as proof that it is protected against the most popular security attacks. Then, by Scyther tool, we implement the designed protocol security and correctness.

1. *User anonymity and un-traceability* [66]: An attacker cannot catch or find the device's private identity as ($\mathbf{ID_s}$,$\mathbf{ID_f}$,$\mathbf{ID_{Bc}}$), which is transmitted in the public channel during the passing parameter and authentication frames. In the proposed protocol, the adversary cannot extract real identity (Sensor Nodes ($\mathbf{ID_s}$), Fog Nodes($\mathbf{ID_F}$), Blockchain ($\mathbf{ID_{Bc}}$)). These identities are dependent on

Reference	First node	Second node	Third node	Communication overhead
[62]	$3L_{ID} + L_{FE} + 6L_h + L_T$	$L_{ID} + L_{FE} + 11L_h + L_T$	$L_{ID} + 2L_h + L_T$	$5L_{ID} + 2\ L_{FE} + 19L_h + 3L_T$
[63]	$L_{ID} + 7L_h + L_T$	$L_{ECC} + L_{E/D} + L_{FE} + 5L_h + 3L_T$	$L_{ECC} + 2L_h + L_T$	$L_{ID} + 2L_{ECC} + L_{E/D} + L_{FE} + 14L_h + 5L_T$
[64]	$L_{ECC} + 5L_h$	$2L_{ECC} + 10L_h$	$L_{ECC} + 2L_{FE}$	$4L_{ECC} + 15L_h + 2L_{FE}$
[65]	$L_{ECC} + 4L_{E/D} + 3L_h + 1L_T$	$2L_{ECC} + 2L_h + 2L_T$	$L_{ECC} + L_h + L_T$	$4L_{ECC} + 4L_{E/D} + 6L_h + 4L_T$
[61]	$2L_{ECC} + 4L_h + L_T$	$3L_{ECC} + 10L_h + 2L_T$	$L_{ECC} + 2L_h + L_T$	$6L_{ECC} + 16L_h + 4L_T$
Our proposed	$2L_{ECC} + 2L_h + 2L_{E/D}$	$6L_{ECC} + 2L_h + 2T_{E/D}$	$L_{ID} + 2L_{ECC} + 2L_h + 3T_{E/D}$	$3L_{ID} + 6L_{ECC} + 5L_h + 8T_{E/D}$

Table 14.
Comparison of computational overhead.

Reference	First node	Second node	Third node	Communication overhead (bits)
[62]	1152	1952	384	3488
[63]	1280	1184	510	2976
[64]	960	1920	416	3296
[65]	1184	704	352	2240
[61]	992	2144	510	3646
Our proposed	480	800	640	1920

Table 15.
Comparison of communication overheads in bits.

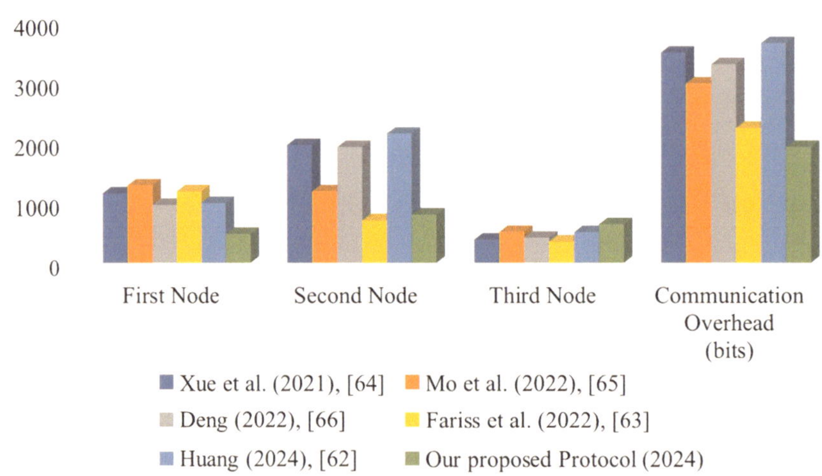

Figure 9.
The display of comparison of communication overhead (bits).

encryption and decryption methods when passing parameters between nodes are encrypted into $Enc_{K.SF}$, $Enc_{K.FBc}$, $Enc_{K.BcF}$, $Enc_{K.BcS}$ between nodes.

2. *Message integrity and denial of service-dos attack* [67]: It is a form of attack that aims to take down a computer or network and render it inaccessible. DoS attacks work by overwhelmingly "Flooding" the target with traffic or giving it information that causes the target to break down. The result of the DoS attack is to prevent legal users of the service. To execute a DoS Attack, it can select an open port that should be found, and then, lots of traffic need to be sent since this attack can lead to serious energy depletion at the nodes. The proposed protocol that can prevent a DoS attack is by using check integrity between nodes $\mathbf{A_1 = H_2(X_s \| Y_s \| C_1)}$, $\mathbf{A_2 = H_2(X_s \| Y_s \| X_f \| Y_f \| C_2)}$, $\mathbf{A_3 = H_2(X_s \| Y_s \| X_f \| Y_f \| X_{Bc} \| Y_{Bc} \| C_3)}$, **and** $\mathbf{A_4 = H_2(X_s \| Y_s \| X_f \| Y_f \| X_{Bc} \| Y_{Bc} \| C_4)}$.

3. *Distributed denial of service (DDoS) "legitimate user attacks"* [68]: The attacker is using a flood of a server with internet traffic to prevent users from connected to online services and sites. The proposed protocol can prevent the user by using authorization registration phase and verification for every transaction between nodes by using integrity such as $A_1 = H_2(X_s \| Y_s \| C_1)$ and verifications these transactions when access into another side $A_1?? = H_2(X_s \| Y_s \| C_1)$ and so on the A_2 and A_3 And A_4.

4. *Key-compromise impersonation resilience* [69]: It is defined to be the property that, in any session, the compromise of a user's long-term private key does not enable the attacker to impersonate any non-compromised intended user to the user whose key has been compromised. Resistance to such attacks is often seen as desirable.

   As the formula

$$\begin{aligned} &\partial_{SF} = X_f\varnothing_A + \varnothing_A Y_f;\ \partial_{SBc} = X_{Bc}\varnothing_A + Y_{Bc}\varnothing_A;\ \partial_{FBc} = X_{Bc}\varnothing_B + Y_{Bc}\varnothing_B; \\ &\partial_{BcF} = X_f\varnothing_B + Y_f\varnothing_B;\ \partial_{BcS} = \varnothing_{BC}X_s + \varnothing_{Bc}Y_s \end{aligned} \tag{1}$$

   In this scenario, the attacker corrupts the private key in every node of the sensor node and fog node to impersonate the Blockchain node and to cheat the sensor device and fog device. Although the attacker can compute the sensor device's public key, it is still not able to derive ($\boldsymbol{\partial_{SF}}$, $\boldsymbol{\partial_{SBc}}$, ∂_{FBc}, ∂_{BcF}, and ∂_{BcS}) because it needs the private key ($\mathbf{r_s, r_f, r_{Bc}}$) to decrypt the cipher text $\mathbf{C_2, C_3, C_4}$. As a result, the attacker will not be allowed to compute the common secret **SK** between nodes.

5. *Perfect forward privacy* [70]: If the SK is compromised, an attacker could decrypt past messages, meaning if the attacker stored the corresponding ciphertext. It is defined to be the property that the compromise of the long-term private keys of some (but not all) intended users in a successfully ended session does not compromise the session key established in that session.

   Even if the attacker can steal the long-term private keys of the node of the system, the previously created shared secret keys are compromised. Indeed, the random values are also requested for the creation of these session keys $\mathbf{r_S}$, $\mathbf{r_F}$, $\mathbf{r_{Bc}}$, which change at each session.

Suppose that $\mathbf{y_F}$ of $\mathbf{ID_f}$ or $\boldsymbol{m_{Bc}}$ of $\mathbf{ID_{Bc}}$ is compromised and A acquires $\boldsymbol{x_S}$, $\mathbf{ID_S}$. To calculate the correct $\mathbf{SK{=}H_2(ID_s, ID_f, ID_{Bc}, X_s, Y_s, X_f, Y_f, X_{Bc}, Y_{Bc}, \varnothing_A, \varnothing_B, \varnothing_{Bc}, \partial_{SF}, \partial_{SBc}, \partial_{FBc})}$, A is required to calculate $\mathbf{Y_F}$ or $\mathbf{X}_{Bc}$; this type is working against resistance to tampering attacks.

6. *Key control attack:* The proposed technique computes the common secret SK using the private keys of all entities and random integers. As a result, even if one of the entities is corrupted, the attacker will still be unable to discover the SK. In the proposed protocol, neither party can alone control the session key, in which using identifications for perusers as ($\mathbf{ID_s}$) and ($\mathbf{ID_f}$) and ($\mathbf{ID_{Bc}}$). While using selected arbitrary numbers m_s, n_s and m_f, n_f and m_{Bc}, n_{Bc} as private keys to form common session keys. The session key $\mathbf{SK{=}H_2(ID_s, ID_f, ID_{Bc}, X_s, Y_s, X_f, Y_f, X_{Bc}, Y_{Bc}, \varnothing_A, \varnothing_B, \varnothing_{Bc}, \partial_{SF}, \partial_{SBc}, \partial_{FBc})}$, is resistant to Denning-Sacco attacks to this type is create the SK by using an Ephemeral Public Key and Ephemeral private Key at the same time; in addition, the data is transmitted by Quantum channel.

7. *Unknown key share (UKS) resistance* [71]: The reliability of AKE (Authentication Key Establishment) protocols is resistance to the UKS attack as a major security mechanism. In actuality, ($\mathbf{ID_s}$) and ($\mathbf{ID_f}$) and ($\mathbf{ID_{Bc}}$) are a contribution by the same actual identity together by generating itself by the session key (SK). As the session key $\mathbf{SK{=}H_2(ID_s, ID_f, ID_c, X_s, Y_s, X_f, Y_f, X_{Bc}, Y_{Bc}, \varnothing_A, \varnothing_B, \varnothing_{Bc}, \partial_{SF}, \partial_{SBc}, \partial_{FBc})}$, this type of attack is resistant to smart card loss attacks and offline guessing attacks.

8. *Man-in-the-middle attack:* In this type, the attacker will retrieve and modify shared communication messages in the authentication key exchange protocol as the adversary (A) concealed from (F) to (Bc) and the other side from (Bc) to (F). The proposed protocol resistance to this attack derives from the pre-request key agreement, the Super Singular into Quantum certificate protocol was used.

   Each entity's certificate is generated using this method. Furthermore, the private key of the KGC (Key Generation Center) is used for the organization installed in the implicit certificate.

9. *Session key leakage:* The session secrets are generated since the session secrets depend on both random numbers and private keys, and they differ from session to session since the reliability of the other session keys is not influenced by the leaking of one key in the session key. By using an Ephemeral Private Key (Secret integer) such as (m_s, n_s, m_f, n_f, m_{Bc}, n_{Bc}) and an Ephemeral Public Key such as (X_s, Y_s, X_f, Y_f, X_{Bc}, Y_{Bc}). This type of attack can prevent the resistance to spoofed user attacks and internal attacks.

10. *Resistance to replay attack:* This attack refers to sending an old message by the attacker repeatedly. Suppose that the attacker is using the old message as M_1= ($\mathbf{E_A}$, $\mathbf{X_s}$, $\mathbf{Y_s}$, C_1, A_1). The Fog node encrypts this message by $C_1{=}Enc_{KSF}$ ($ID_s||\varnothing_A$), then decrypts into the fog node the same message ($ID_s||\varnothing_A$) = Dec_{KSF} (C_1). Then compare with P_s?? = $H(ID_s|| d_s)d_s + K$, to compare $\mathbf{P_S}$ (obtained from

decryption) with Sensor node. Also, encrypt the value $C_2 = Enc_{K.FBc}(ID_s || ID_f || \varnothing_A || \varnothing_B || \partial_{SF})$ and then decrypt in the Blockchain $(ID_s || ID_f || \varnothing_A || \varnothing_B || \partial_{SF}) = Dec_{K.FBc}(C_2)$ and verify by $P_f?? = H(ID_f || d_f)d_f + K$; hence, encrypt the $C_3 = Enc_{K.BcF}(ID_{Bc} || ID_f || \varnothing_{Bc} || \partial_{FBc})$ and $C_4 = Enc_{K.BcS}(ID_{Bc} || ID_s || \varnothing_{Bc} || \partial_{SBc})$.

11. *Mutual authentication:* At the authentication between nodes, it must validate messages, mutual authentication is the verification of validity at the same time by $A_1 = H_2(X_s || Y_s || C_1)$, $P_s?? = H(ID_s || d_s)d_s + K$ upon receiving from cloud sensors checks the validity $A_2 = H_2(X_s || Y_s || X_f || Y_f || C_2)$. Then FN checks the validity of Bc by $A_2 = H_2(X_s || Y_s || X_f || Y_f || C_2)$, $P_f?? = H(ID_f || d_f)d_f + K$. Lastly, in (SN) upon receiving (FN) checks the validity and checks to validate. $A_3 = H_2(X_f || Y_f || X_{Bc} || Y_{Bc} || C_3)$ and $A_4 = H_2(X_s || Y_s || X_{Bc} || Y_{Bc} || C_4)$ and check to validate.

Table 16 shows the security features comparison and how our proposed protocol (Post-Quantum Super Singular Key Agreement by Hyperelliptic Curve Cryptography) outperforms the other related protocol encryption algorithms.

7.4 Formal security verification *via* ProVerif

We utilize ProVerif, a widely recognized automated tool for the formal verification of cryptographic protocols, to validate the security properties of our proposed protocol. ProVerif is capable of modeling various cryptographic primitives and protocols, analyzing their security properties, and detecting potential vulnerabilities. It can implement the properties of the security in the proposed protocol such as reference [72].

ProVerif employs a process calculus called the applied pi-calculus, which allows it to model the behavior of cryptographic protocols in a formal and rigorous manner. The tool translates the protocol description into a set of logical queries that can be verified for security properties such as confidentiality, authenticity, and integrity.

Security features	Reference					Our proposed
	[62]	[63]	[64]	[65]	[61]	
Year	2021	2022	2022	2022	2022	2024
Perfect forward privacy:	×	×	×	×	✓	✓
Resist KSSTI attacks	×	×	×	✓	✓	✓
Resist internal privilege attacks	✓	×	✓	×	✓	✓
Resist offline dictionary attacks	✓	✓	✓	✓	✓	✓
Clock synchronization	✓	×	✓	×	✓	✓
Anonymity	×	✓	✓	✓	✓	✓
Resist MITM attacks	×	×	✓	✓	✓	✓
Resist user registration attacks	×	✓	✓	✓	✓	✓
Resistance to replay attack	×	×	×	×	×	✓
Resistance key-compromise	×	×	×	×	×	✓
Loss of information	×	×	×	×	×	✓

Table 16.
Comparison of security features.

ProVerif can handle an extensive range of cryptographic primitives, including symmetric and asymmetric encryption, hash functions, and digital signatures.

For our protocol, we model key aspects in ProVerif, including the main entities involved (such as sensor nodes, fog nodes, and Blockchain nodes), the types of messages exchanged (including their formats and the cryptographic operations applied to them), and the specific security goals we aim to verify, such as the secrecy of session keys and the authenticity of messages.

Our primary verification goals include ensuring the confidentiality of sensitive information like session keys, verifying the authenticity of entities to prevent impersonation attacks, and maintaining the integrity of messages exchanged between participants to ensure they are not tampered with during transmission.

ProVerif is a powerful tool for analyzing the security of cryptographic protocols, offering key features such as automated analysis of security properties, broad support for various protocols (including key exchange, authentication, and secure communication), abstract modeling for high-level reasoning about security properties, and counterexample generation to help understand failures when a protocol does not meet a security property.

In the following, we have dispelled analysis of the verification and authentication proposed protocol:

1. *Definitions:* Define types and functions for keys and messages, and encryption and decryption functions.

```
free ChSec: channel [private]. (*secure channel between M, GSC and D*).
free ChPub: channel. (*public channel between M, GSC and D*)
free IDs:bitstring.
free IDc:bitstring.
free IDf:bitstring.
free IDBC:bitstring.
free Phib:bitstring.
free Pa:bitstring.
free ds:bitstring.
free df:bitstring.
free Pc:bitstring.
free C4:bitstring.
free A4:bitstring.
free nbc:bitstring.
free Qc:bitstring.
free mbc:bitstring.
free Pf:bitstring.
free Ps:bitstring.
free Qa:bitstring.
free IDbc:bitstring.
free sigmafbc:bitstring.
free Pb:bitstring.
free Qb:bitstring.
free sigmasbc:bitstring.
free phic:bitstring.
free Yf:bitstring.
free nf:bitstring.
free mf:bitstring.
free phibc:bitstring.
free SK:bitstring [private].
free K:bitstring [private].
```

```
free PB : bitstring.
fun H2(bitstring): bitstring.
fun Decfbc(bitstring):bitstring.
fun Decbcd(bitstring):bitstring.
fun Decsf(bitstring):bitstring.
fun Concat(bitstring,bitstring) : bitstring.
fun ECPM(bitstring,bitstring) : bitstring.
fun mul(bitstring,bitstring) : bitstring.
fun add(bitstring , bitstring) : bitstring.
fun Decbcs(bitstring):bitstring.
fun Encsf(bitstring) : bitstring.
fun Encfbc(bitstring) : bitstring.
fun Encbcf(bitstring) : bitstring.
fun Encbcs(bitstring) : bitstring.
```

2. *Events and queries:* Verify that for each identifier, The Events are used to mark significant points in the protocol for verification purposes. Queries are used to specify the security properties to be verified, such as ensuring that certain events occur in the correct order.

```
query id:bitstring; inj-event(end_s(IDs)) ==> inj-event(start_s(IDs)).
query id:bitstring; inj-event(end_f(IDf)) ==> inj-event(start_f(IDf)).
query id:bitstring; inj-event(end_BC(IDBC)) ==> inj-event(start_BC
(IDBC)).
query attacker(SK).
event start_s(bitstring).
event end_s(bitstring).
event start_f(bitstring).
event end_f(bitstring).
event start_BC(bitstring).
event end_BC(bitstring).
```

3. *Process definitions:* Processes are used to describe the behavior of each node in the protocol. Each node's actions, such as sending and receiving messages, encrypting and decrypting data, and event logging, are defined in these processes.

```
let ps=
event start_s(IDs);
new ms:bitstring;
new Pa:bitstring;
let Xs=ECPM(ms,Pa) in
new ns:bitstring;
let Ys=ECPM(ns,Qa) in
```

4. *Parallel composition and replication:* ProVerif supports parallel composition and replication of processes, allowing the modeling of multiple instances of protocol participants running concurrently.

```
process ((!pBC) | (!pf)| (!ps))
```

5. *The result:* The results will indicate whether the queries hold or if there are potential security vulnerabilities in the protocol. For every transaction between sensors, Fog, and Blockchain each "id," the occurrence of the "end_s" event implies the "start_s" event occurred, ensuring that sensor protocol execution steps are authenticated. And for "end_f" and "end_BC," it confirms that fog and Blockchain protocol steps are authenticated as well (True). Otherwise, when the result is (False), the protocol is having issues.

```
Verification summary:
Query inj-event (end_s (IDs[])) ==> inj-event(starts (IDs[])) is true.
Query inj-event (end_f (IDf[])) ==> inj-event(start_f (IDf[])) is true.
Query inj-event (end_BC (IDBC[])) ==> inj-event(start_BC (IDBC[])) is true.
Query not attacker (SK[]) is true.
----------------------------------------------------
```

The formal verification using ProVerif confirms that our proposed protocol meets the desired security properties. The confidentiality of session keys, the authenticity of the communicating parties, and the integrity of the messages are all maintained. This formal verification provides a high level of assurance that our protocol is secure against common cryptographic attacks.

8. Conclusions

Wireless Sensor Networks (WSNs) play a crucial role in delivering timely and accurate data, particularly for continuous surveillance in challenging outdoor environments. The collaborative data collection facilitated by distributed sensing enhances fault resilience and scalability, making WSNs robust in extreme situations. The integration of Post-Quantum Cryptography involves advanced techniques derived from complex mathematical problems, addressing challenges for both classical and quantum computers. The overarching goal is to develop encryption and digital signature systems resilient against potential quantum attacks. Presently, the most effective strategy for mitigating quantum threats involves the development of robust encryption methods resistant to quantum computing.

Public Key Infrastructure (PKI) remains a prominent encryption technique, with its core principles persisting in the domain of Post-Quantum Cryptography. However, Post-Quantum Cryptography comes with inherent constraints, such as the need for substantial key sizes, posing potential performance challenges. Recognizing the vulnerability of lightweight cryptography designed for resource-constrained devices to quantum attacks, researchers are dedicated to crafting efficient and lightweight post-quantum cryptographic systems suitable for deployment on such devices. The ongoing efforts of researchers play a pivotal role in fostering the adoption and seamless integration of post-quantum cryptography into Internet of Things (IoT) networks.

In the context of WSNs, post-quantum Public Key Infrastructure emerges as a crucial tool for securing communication channels between nodes. This technique encompasses the encryption of data packets and node authentication, effectively preventing unauthorized access and tampering. The continuous collaboration and advancements in post-quantum cryptography, particularly in lightweight applications, promise enhanced security and resilience in the evolving landscape of IoT networks.

We have conducted a comprehensive literature review of the state of the art in quantum cryptography applied to WSNs using PKI. We identified the main trends, challenges, and proposed solutions in the literature, highlighting the evolution and integration of new cryptographic techniques to address emerging threats. Our main contribution lies in the proposal of an innovative security protocol based on Supersingular Hyperelliptic Curve Cryptography (HECC) with a reduced key size. This protocol not only improves the energy efficiency and performance of WSNs but also provides robust resistance to quantum attacks, making it highly relevant in the context of IoT. Additionally, we formally validated the security of our protocol using the ProVerif tool, ensuring the confidentiality, authenticity, and integrity of communications in the proposed system.

Future perspectives in cryptography for WSNs include the implementation and testing of post-quantum algorithms in real environments, optimizing protocols to further reduce energy consumption and latency, and integration with emerging technologies such as fog and edge computing. Furthermore, the continuous evolution of quantum attacks requires constant vigilance and adaptation of cryptographic schemes to ensure long-term data protection.

In summary, our literature review and presented innovations provide a solid framework for future research and development in the security of wireless sensor networks, ensuring their sustainability and efficiency in an increasingly interconnected environment threatened by new forms of attack.

Acknowledgements

Under Project UAL18-TIC-A025-A, University of Almeria, Ministry of Economy, Knowledge, Business and University, and the European Regional Development Fund (FEDER); Andalusian Regional Government through the Electronics, Communication, and Telemedicine Research Group of the University of Almeria, Spain; and in part by the European Union FEDER Program and CIAMBITAL Group.

Conflict of interest

The authors declare no conflict of interest.

Author details

Mohamad Al-Samhouri[1], Nuria Novas[2*], Maher Abur-rous[3] and
Jose Antonio Gazquez[2]

1 Department of Computer Science, University of Almeria, CIAMBITAL, CEIA3, Almeria, Spain

2 Engineering Department, University of Almeria, CIAMBITAL, CEIA3, Almeria, Spain

3 College of Technological Innovation, Zayed University, Abu Dhabi, United Arab Emirate

*Address all correspondence to: nnovas@ual.es

References

[1] Faris M, Mahmud MN, Salleh MFM, Alnoor A. Wireless sensor network security: A recent review based on state-of-the-art works. International Journal of Engineering Business Management. 2023;**15**:1-29. DOI: 10.1177/18479790231157220

[2] Fahmy HMA. WSNs applications. In: Concepts, Applications, Experimentation and Analysis of Wireless Sensor Networks. Switzerland: Springer Nature; 2023. pp. 67-242. DOI: 10.1007/978-3-031-20709-9_3

[3] Adu-Manu KS, Engmann F, Sarfo-Kantanka G, Baiden GE, Dulemordzi BA. WSN protocols and security challenges for environmental monitoring applications: A survey. Journal of Sensors. 2022;**2022**:1628537. DOI: 10.1155/2022/1628537

[4] Ramesh MV et al. Achieving sustainability through smart city applications: Protocols, systems and solutions using IoT and wireless sensor network. CSI Transactions on ICT. 2020; **8**(2):213-230. DOI: 10.1007/s40012-020-00285-5

[5] Aponte-Luis J, Gómez-Galán JA, Gómez-Bravo F, Sánchez-Raya M, Alcina-Espigado J, Teixido-Rovira PM. An efficient wireless sensor network for industrial monitoring and control. Sensors (Switzerland) (MDPI AG). Jan 2018;**18**(1):182. DOI: 10.3390/s18010182

[6] Ertam F, Kilincer IF, Yaman O, Sengur A. A new IoT application for dynamic WiFi based wireless sensor network. In: International Conference on Electrical Engineering, ICEE 2020. 2020. pp. 17-20. DOI: 10.1109/ICEE49691.2020.9249771

[7] Perera K, Ranidu J, Gunasekera K. Towards an adaptive communication framework for smart devices. In: MERCon 2022 - Moratuwa Engineering Research Conference, Proceedings. Moratuwa, Sri Lanka; 2022. pp. 1-6. DOI: 10.1109/MERCon55799.2022.9906272

[8] Evangelakos EA, Kandris D, Rountos D, Tselikis G, Anastasiadis E. Energy sustainability in wireless sensor networks: An analytical survey. Journal of Low Power Electronics and Applications. 2022;**12**(4):65. DOI: 10.3390/jlpea12040065

[9] Gurram GV, Shariff NC, Biradar RL. A secure energy aware meta-heuristic routing protocol (SEAMHR) for sustainable IoT-wireless sensor network (WSN). Theoretical Computer Science. 2022;**930**:63-76. DOI: 10.1016/j.tcs.2022.07.011

[10] Singh S, Nandan AS, Malik A, Kumar R, Awasthi LK, Kumar N. A GA-based sustainable and secure green data communication method using IoT-enabled WSN in healthcare. IEEE Internet of Things Journal. 2022;**9**(10): 7481-7490. DOI: 10.1109/JIOT.2021.3108875

[11] Shen C-C, Srisathapornphat C, Jaikaeo C. Sensor information networking architecture and applications. IEEE Personal Communications. 2001;**8**(4):52-59. DOI: 10.1109/98.944004

[12] Mukherjee N, Neogy S, Roy S. Building wireless sensor networks, theoretical and practical perspectives [book review]. IEEE Wireless Communications. 2016;**23**(2):4-5. DOI: 10.1109/mwc.2016.7462477

[13] Rathee A, Singh R, Nandini A. Wireless sensor network- challenges and

possibilities. International Journal of Computers and Applications. 2016; **140**(2):1-15. DOI: 10.5120/ijca2016909221

[14] Fahmy HMA. Concepts, Applications, Experimentation and Analysis of Wireless Sensor Networks. Netherlands: Third. Springer; 2023

[15] Parween S, Hussain SZ. A review on cross-layer design approach in WSN by different techniques. Advances in Science, Technology and Engineering Systems. 2020;**5**(4):741-754. DOI: 10.25046/AJ050488

[16] Khalifeh A, Abid H, Darabkh KA. Optimal cluster head positioning algorithm for wireless sensor networks. Sensors (Switzerland). 2020;**20**(13): 1-26. DOI: 10.3390/s20133719

[17] Younis O, Fahmy S. HEED: A hybrid, energy-efficient, distributed clustering approach for ad hoc sensor networks. IEEE Transactions on Mobile Computing. 2004;**3**(4):366-379. DOI: 10.1109/TMC.2004.41

[18] Pal S, Bhattacharyya D, Tomar GS, Kim T. Wireless sensor networks and its routing protocols: A comparative study. In: Proceedings - 2010 International Conference on Computational Intelligence and Communication Networks, CICN 2010. Bhopal; 2010. pp. 314-319. DOI: 10.1109/CICN.2010.71

[19] Zhou H, Wu Y, Xie G. EDFM: A stable election protocol based on energy dissipation forecast method for clustered heterogeneous wireless sensor networks. In: Proceedings - 5th International Conference on Wireless Communications, Networking and Mobile Computing, WiCOM 2009. Beijing, China; 2009. pp. 20-23. DOI: 10.1109/WICOM.2009.5304152

[20] Kashaf A, Javaid N, Khan ZA, Khan IA. TSEP: Threshold-sensitive stable election protocol for WSNs. In: Proceedings - 10th International Conference on Frontiers of Information Technology, FIT 2012. Islamabad, Pakistan; 2012. pp. 164-168. DOI: 10.1109/FIT.2012.37

[21] Ben Yagouta A et al. Multiple Mobile sinks for quality of service improvement in large-scale wireless sensor networks. Sensors (Basel). 2023;**23**(20):1-23. DOI: 10.3390/s23208534

[22] Chen K-H, Huang J-M, Hsiao C-C. CHIRON: An energy-efficient chain-based hierarchical routing protocol in wireless sensor networks. In: 2009 Wireless Telecommunications Symposium, WTS 2009. 2009. pp. 1-5. DOI: 10.1109/WTS.2009.5068960

[23] Tabassum N, Ehsanul Q, Mamun K, Urano Y. COSEN: A chain oriented sensor network for efficient data collection. In: Proceedings - Third International Conference onInformation Technology: New Generations, ITNG 2006. Vol. 2006. Las Vegas, NV, USA; 2006. pp. 262-267. DOI: 10.1109/ITNG.2006.44

[24] Alenizi F, Rana O. Minimising delay and energy in online dynamic fog systems. Computer Science and Information Technologies. 2020;**14**: 139-158. DOI: 10.5121/csit.2020.101513

[25] Del-Pozo-Puñal E, García-Carballeira F, Camarmas-Alonso D. A scalable simulator for cloud, fog and edge computing platforms with mobility support. Future Generation Computer Systems. 2023;**144**:117-130. DOI: 10.1016/j.future.2023.02.010

[26] Alharbi HA, Aldossary M. Energy-efficient edge-fog-cloud architecture for

IoT-based smart agriculture environment. IEEE Access. 2021;**9**: 110480-110492. DOI: 10.1109/ACCESS.2021.3101397

[27] Yousefpour A et al. All one needs to know about fog computing and related edge computing paradigms: A complete survey. Journal of Systems Architecture. 2019;**98**(December 2018): 289-330. DOI: 10.1016/j.sysarc.2019.02.009

[28] Maciel P et al. A survey on reliability and availability modeling of edge, fog, and cloud computing. Journal of Reliable Intelligent Environments. 2022;**8**(3): 227-245. DOI: 10.1007/s40860-021-00154-1

[29] Marquesone RDFP, da Silva ÉA, Gonzalez NM, Langona K, Goya WA, Frota Redígolo F, et al. Towards bandwidth optimization in fog computing using FACE framework. In: CLOSER 2017 - Proceedings of the 7th International Conference on Cloud Computing and Services Science. Porto, Portugal; 2017. pp. 463-470. DOI: 10.5220/0006303804910498

[30] Barker E, Barker WC. Recommendation for Key Management. Gaithersburg, MD: National Institute of Standards and Technology; May 2019

[31] Szymoniak S. Key distribution and authentication protocols in wireless sensor networks: A survey. ACM Computing Surveys. 2024;**56**(6):1-31. DOI: 10.1145/3638043

[32] Sen J. Cryptography and key management schemes for wireless sensor networks. In: Wireless Sensor Networks - Design, Applications and Challenges. IntechOpen; 2023. pp. 1-24. DOI: 10.5772/intechopen.112277

[33] Distributed denial-of-service attacks. In: Cloud Control Systems. Elsevier; 2020. pp. 51-76

[34] Kakani PP. Data Aggregation and Gathering Transmission in Wireless Sensor Networks: A Survey PHANI PRIYA KAKANI THESIS WORK2011–2013 Master of Electrical Engineering: Specialization inEmbedded Systems; 2013

[35] Hu YC, Perrig A. Wormhole attacks in wireless networks. IEEE Journal on Selected Areas in Communications. 2006;**24**(2):370-379. DOI: 10.1109/JSAC.2005.861394

[36] Ghugar U, Pradhan J. Study of black hole attack in wireless sensor networks. International Journal of Advanced Computer Science and Applications. 2017;**5**(1):1-3

[37] Luo X, Ji X, Park M-S. Location privacy against traffic analysis attacks in wireless sensor networks. In: 2010 International Conference on Information Science and Applications, ICISA 2010. Seoul, Korea (South); 2010. pp. 1-6. DOI: 10.1109/ICISA.2010.5480564

[38] Dai HN, Wang Q, Li D, Wong RCW. On eavesdropping attacks in wireless sensor networks with directional antennas. International Journal of Distributed Sensor Networks. 2013;**9**(8): 1-13. DOI: 10.1155/2013/760834

[39] Gupta SC, Singh B, Amjad M, Gopianand M, Bhuvaneswari E. Security enhancement using quantum cryptography in {WSN}. In: 2021 7th International Conference on Advanced Computing and Communication Systems (ICACCS), Coimbatore, India. IEEE; Mar 2021

[40] Navarrete Á, Zapatero V, Curty M. Quantum key distribution protocols. In: Photonic Quantum Technologies: Science and Applications: Volumes 1–2. Vol. 1. Wiley; 2023. DOI: 10.1002/9783527837427.ch5

[41] Stebila D, Mosca M, Lütkenhaus N. The case for quantum key distribution. Lecture Notes of the Institute for Computer Sciences, Social Informatics and Telecommunications Engineering. 2010;**36 LNICST**:283-296. DOI: 10.1007/978-3-642-11731-2_35

[42] Balamurugan C, Singh K, Ganesan G, Rajarajan M. Post-quantum and code-based cryptography—some prospective research directions. Cryptography (MDPI AG). Dec 2021;**5**(4):38. DOI: 10.20944/PREPRINTS202104.0734.V1

[43] Kumar M. Quantum Computing and Post-Quaantum Cryptography. Society for Makers, Artist, Researchers and Technologists; 2021. DOI: 10.15864/ijiip.2405

[44] Yang Z, Alfauri H, Farkiani B, Jain R, Pietro RD, Erbad A. A survey and comparison of post-quantum and quantum blockchains. IEEE Communication Surveys and Tutorials (Institute of Electrical and Electronics Engineers (IEEE)). 2024;**26**(2):967-1002

[45] Bennett CH, Brassard G. Quantum cryptography: Public key distribution and coin tossing. Theoretical Computer Science. 2014;**560**(P1):7-11. DOI: 10.1016/j.tcs.2014.05.025

[46] Bennett CH, Brassard G, Mermin ND. Quantum cryptography without Bell's theorem. Physical Review Letters. 1992;**68**(5):557-559. DOI: 10.1103/PhysRevLett.68.557

[47] Ekert AK. Quantum cryptography and Bell's theorem. Physical Review Letters. 1991;**67**(7):661-663. DOI: 10.1007/978-1-4615-3386-3_34

[48] Sabani M, Savvas I, Poulakis D, Makris G. Quantum key distribution: Basic protocols and threats. In: Proceedings of the 26th Pan-Hellenic Conference on Informatics, Athens, Greece. New York, NY, USA: ACM; Nov 2022. pp. 383-388. DOI: 10.1145/3575879.3576022

[49] Usenko VC, Grosshans F. Unidimensional continuous-variable quantum key distribution. Physical Review A - Atomic, Molecular, and Optical Physics. 2015;**92**(6):1-6. DOI: 10.1103/PhysRevA.92.062337

[50] Lo HK, Curty M, Qi B. Measurement-device-independent quantum key distribution. Physical Review Letters. 2012;**108**(13):1-5. DOI: 10.1103/PhysRevLett.108.130503

[51] van Tilborg HCA, Jajodia S. Encyclopedia of Cryptography and Security. Boston, MA: Springer US; 2011. DOI: 10.1007/978-1-4419-5906-5

[52] Hoffstein J, Pipher J, Silverman JH. An Introduction to Mathematical Cryptography. Undergraduate Texts in Mathematics. New York, NY: Springer; Dec 2008

[53] McEliece RJ. A Public Key Cryptosystem Based on Algebraic Coding Theory. 1978. Available from: https://api.semanticscholar.org/CorpusID:56502909

[54] Jao D, De Feo L. Towards quantum-resistant cryptosystems from Supersingular elliptic curve isogenies. In: Yang B-Y, editor. Post-Quantum Cryptography. PQCrypto 2011. Lecture

Notes in Computer Science. Vol. 7071. Berlin Heidelberg: Springer; 2011. pp. 19-34. DOI: 10.1007/978-3-642-25405-5_2

[55] Naresh VS, Reddi S, Murthy NVES. Provable secure lightweight multiple shared key agreement based on hyper elliptic curve Diffie–Hellman for wireless sensor networks. Journal of Information Security. 2020;**29**(1): 1-13. DOI: 10.1080/19393555.2019.1708516

[56] Vijayakumar P, Vijayalakshmi V, Zayaraz G. Comparative study of Hyperelliptic curve cryptosystem over prime field and its survey. International Journal of Hybrid Information Technology. 2014;7(1):137-146. DOI: 10.14257/ijhit.2014.7.1.11

[57] Pelzl J, Wollinger T, Guajardo J, Paar C. Hyperelliptic curve cryptosystems: Closing the performance gap to elliptic curves. In: Lecture Notes in Computer Science. Berlin, Heidelberg: Springer; 2003. pp. 351-365. DOI: 10.1007/978-3-540-45238-6_28

[58] Jao D, Azarderakhsh R, Campagna M, Costello C, De Feo L, Hess B, et al. Supersingular Isogeny Key Encapsulation; 2018. DOI: 10.13140/RG.2.2.26543.07847 [Unpublished]

[59] De Feo L, Jao D, Plût J. Towards quantum-resistant cryptosystems from supersingular elliptic curve isogenies. Journal of Mathematical Cryptology. 2014;**8**(3):209-247. DOI: 10.1515/jmc-2012-0015

[60] Costello C. Supersingular isogeny key exchange for beginners. In: Selected Areas in Cryptography–SAC 2019: 26th International Conference. Vol. 11959 LNCS. Cham; 2019. pp. 21-50. DOI: 10.1007/978-3-030-38471-5_2

[61] Huang W. ECC-based three-factor authentication and key agreement scheme for wireless sensor networks. Scientific Reports. 2024;**14**(1):1-20. DOI: 10.1038/s41598-024-52134-z

[62] Xue L, Huang Q, Zhang S, Huang H, Wang W. A lightweight three-factor authentication and key agreement scheme for multigateway WSNs in IoT. Security and Communication Networks. 2021;**2021**(3300769):1-15. DOI: 10.1155/2021/3300769

[63] Mo J, Hu Z, Shen W. A provably secure three-factor authentication protocol based on Chebyshev chaotic mapping for wireless sensor network. IEEE Access. 2022;**10**:12137-12152. DOI: 10.1109/ACCESS.2022.3146393

[64] Deng D. Research on Key Technologies of Authentication and Secret Key Management Based on Non-traditional Certificates in WSN. Univ. Electron. Sci. Technol.; 2022

[65] Fariss M, El Gafif H, Toumanari A. A lightweight ECC-based three-factor mutual authentication and key agreement protocol for WSNs in IoT. International Journal of Advanced Computer Science and Applications. 2022;**13**(6):491-501. DOI: 10.14569/IJACSA.2022.0130660

[66] Sutrala AK, Obaidat MS, Saha S, Das AK, Alazab M, Park Y. Authenticated key agreement scheme with user anonymity and Untraceability for 5G-enabled Softwarized industrial cyber-physical systems. IEEE Transactions on Intelligent Transportation Systems. 2022;**23**(3): 2316-2330. DOI: 10.1109/TITS.2021.3056704

[67] Matsuura K, Imai H. Protection of authenticated key-agreement protocol

against a denial-of-service attack. In: Proceedings of 1998 International Symposium on Information Theory and its Applications (ISITA'98). Vol. 470. 1998. pp. 466-470

[68] Singh A, Gupta BB. Distributed denial-of-service (DDoS) attacks and defense mechanisms in various web-enabled computing platforms: Issues, challenges, and future research directions. International Journal on Semantic Web and Information Systems (IGI Global). 2022;**18**(1):1-43. DOI: 10.4018/IJSWIS.297143

[69] Strangio MA. On the resilience of key agreement protocols to key compromise impersonation. In: Lecture Notes in Computer Science (Including Subseries Lecture Notes in Artificial Intelligence and Lecture Notes in Bioinformatics). Vol. 4043 LNCS. 2006. pp. 233-247. DOI: 10.1007/11774716_19

[70] Avoine G, Canard S, Ferreira L. Symmetric-key authenticated key exchange (SAKE) with perfect forward secrecy. In: Lecture Notes in Computer Science (Including Subseries Lecture Notes in Artificial Intelligence and Lecture Notes in Bioinformatics). Vol. 12006 LNCS. Springer International Publishing; 2020. pp. 199-224. DOI: 10.1007/978-3-030-40186-3_10

[71] Toorani M, Beheshti A. Cryptanalysis of an efficient signcryption scheme with forward secrecy based on elliptic curve. In: Proceedings of the 2008 International Conference on Computer and Electrical Engineering, ICCEE 2008. Phuket; 2008. pp. 428-432. DOI: 10.1109/ICCEE.2008.147

[72] Dalal N, Shah J, Hisaria K, Jinwala D. A comparative analysis of tools for verification of security protocols. International Journal of Communications, Network and System Sciences. 2010;**03**(10):779-787. DOI: 10.4236/ijcns.2010.310104

Chapter 4

Innovative Vision Glasses for Glaucoma Detection and Management

Kenneth Wong

Abstract

This report delves into the development and application of innovative vision glasses engineered for measuring intraocular pressure (IOP), a crucial aspect of glaucoma monitoring and management. These advanced glasses integrate multiple embedded sensors to offer continuous, real-time data on critical ocular health metrics, facilitating early detection and more effective management of glaucoma. The glasses are equipped with pressure sensors to monitor IOP, focus sensors to evaluate visual acuity, temperature sensors to detect signs of inflammation, and blue light sensors to measure exposure to potentially harmful light. All these components are seamlessly integrated with a microcontroller and a wireless communication system for efficient data transmission and processing. The adoption of this technology promises significant benefits, including increased patient convenience, enhanced accessibility to eye care, and improved early detection capabilities. Moreover, the report features a Python script designed to simulate the glasses' functionality, monitor various parameters, and process data to generate alerts based on predefined thresholds. Looking ahead, the report explores future advancements and broader applications in ophthalmology, such as personalized treatment plans and integration with electronic health records, emphasizing the transformative potential of this technology in advancing eye care and glaucoma management.

Keywords: intraocular pressure, glaucoma monitoring, wearable technology, real-time data, vision glasses, ophthalmology, sensor integration, python script

1. Introduction

Glaucoma is a chronic and progressive eye disease that damages the optic nerve, often associated with elevated intraocular pressure (IOP). It is one of the leading causes of irreversible blindness globally, with the World Health Organization estimating that approximately 80 million people are affected by this condition [1]. The disease progresses slowly and can remain asymptomatic in its early stages, which

IntechOpen

makes early detection crucial for effective management and prevention of vision loss [2]. Without early intervention, glaucoma can lead to severe visual impairment and a significant decline in quality of life [3]. Continuous monitoring of IOP and other ocular parameters is essential for managing glaucoma and preventing its progression.

Current technologies for glaucoma detection include tonometry, perimetry, and optical coherence tomography (OCT). Tonometry measures the pressure inside the eye, which is a key indicator of glaucoma [4]. Perimetry assesses the visual field to detect changes in vision that may be associated with glaucoma progression [5]. OCT provides high-resolution cross-sectional images of the retina and optic nerve, allowing for detailed evaluation of structural changes [6]. Despite their effectiveness, these methods have limitations. They typically require periodic visits to specialized clinics, which can lead to delays in detecting disease progression and hinder timely intervention [7]. Furthermore, these technologies do not provide continuous monitoring, which is essential for capturing fluctuations in IOP and other metrics that may indicate worsening glaucoma.

2. The need for vision glasses

Wearable technology, such as vision glasses equipped with sensors, addresses the limitations of traditional glaucoma detection methods by providing continuous, real-time monitoring. This innovation offers several advantages, including improved convenience for patients and the ability to detect changes in eye health promptly. Vision glasses with embedded sensors can continuously monitor IOP, visual acuity, temperature, and blue light exposure, providing valuable data for early intervention and management [8]. By enabling continuous monitoring, these glasses offer a proactive approach to managing glaucoma, reducing the risk of severe disease progression and enhancing patient outcomes [9].

2.1 Design and development of vision glasses (hardware components)

Pressure Sensors: The vision glasses are equipped with pressure sensors to continuously monitor intraocular pressure. These sensors measure IOP in real time, providing crucial data that can help in detecting fluctuations and potential issues [10]. The integration of advanced pressure sensors ensures accurate and reliable measurement of IOP, which is vital for effective glaucoma management.

Focus Sensors: Focus sensors are incorporated into the glasses to assess changes in visual acuity. These sensors help in monitoring the quality of vision and detecting any deterioration that may be indicative of worsening glaucoma or other eye conditions [11]. By continuously tracking visual acuity, the glasses provide valuable insights into the overall health of the eyes.

Temperature Sensors: The glasses include temperature sensors to monitor eye temperature, which can be an indicator of inflammation or other abnormalities. Changes in eye temperature can signal potential issues that may require further investigation or intervention [12]. Monitoring eye temperature helps in identifying signs of inflammation or infection, contributing to a more comprehensive assessment of eye health.

Blue Light Sensors: Blue light sensors measure exposure to harmful blue light, which can contribute to eye strain and long-term damage. By detecting and quantifying blue light exposure, the glasses help in managing and mitigating the risks associated with prolonged screen time and artificial lighting [13]. This feature is particularly beneficial for individuals who spend significant time in front of screens.

2.2 Microcontroller and data processing

The sensors in the vision glasses are connected to a microcontroller that processes the collected data in real-time. The microcontroller is responsible for integrating data from the various sensors, performing calculations, and analyzing the information to generate meaningful insights [14]. Real-time data processing enables the glasses to provide immediate feedback and alerts based on the monitored parameters. This capability allows for prompt intervention and adjustments to prevent potential issues related to glaucoma [15].

2.3 Wireless communication

Data collected by the vision glasses are transmitted wirelessly to healthcare providers and mobile devices. This feature facilitates remote monitoring, enabling healthcare professionals to access and review patient data from a distance [16]. Wireless communication also allows for seamless integration with electronic health records (EHRs), providing a comprehensive view of the patient's eye health history and facilitating informed decision-making [17]. The ability to transmit data wirelessly enhances the convenience and accessibility of monitoring, making it easier for patients and healthcare providers to stay connected.

3. Features of the vision glasses

3.1 Intraocular pressure monitoring

The vision glasses provide continuous monitoring of intraocular pressure, with real-time data analysis to track fluctuations and identify potential issues [18]. This feature is crucial for managing glaucoma, as elevated IOP is a primary risk factor for the disease. By continuously monitoring IOP, the glasses enable early detection of changes that may require medical attention or adjustments to treatment [19].

3.2 Visual acuity and focus monitoring

The focus sensors in the glasses assess changes in visual acuity, providing valuable information about the quality of vision and eye health [20]. This feature helps in detecting early signs of deterioration that may be associated with glaucoma progression or other eye conditions. Monitoring visual acuity allows for timely intervention and adjustments to treatment plans based on changes in vision [21].

3.3 Temperature and blue light monitoring

The glasses monitor eye temperature and blue light exposure to detect environmental and physiological changes [22]. Changes in eye temperature can indicate inflammation or other issues, while blue light sensors help in managing exposure to harmful light sources. By tracking these parameters, the glasses provide a comprehensive view of eye health and contribute to overall well-being [23].

The vision glasses are equipped with a real-time alert system that generates notifications for abnormal readings and emergency situations [24]. Alerts are sent to users and healthcare providers when parameters exceed predefined thresholds, enabling prompt responses and interventions. This feature ensures that any critical changes in eye health are addressed in a timely manner, reducing the risk of severe complications [25].

3.4 Data logging and cloud integration

Patient data is securely logged and stored in the cloud, allowing for integration with healthcare systems and electronic health records [26]. This capability facilitates comprehensive data analysis and provides healthcare providers with a complete view of the patient's eye health history. Cloud integration also enables data sharing and collaboration among healthcare professionals, enhancing the overall quality of care [27].

4. Simulated data collection and real-time reporting

4.1 Value of simulated data collection

Simulated data collection plays a critical role in validating the functionality of the vision glasses before actual deployment [28, 29]. By generating realistic data within expected ranges, developers can test sensor performance, algorithm accuracy, and system reliability. This process helps in refining the technology, identifying potential issues, and ensuring that the glasses operate effectively under various scenarios [30, 31]. Simulated data also allows for the evaluation of the alert system, ensuring that it responds appropriately to deviations from normal ranges.

4.2 Benefits of real-time reporting

Real-time reporting provides immediate feedback on key ocular parameters, allowing users and healthcare providers to take timely actions based on current data [32]. The ability to monitor parameters such as IOP, visual acuity, and temperature in real-time enhances patient engagement and supports proactive management of eye health [33]. Real-time reporting also facilitates prompt responses to potential issues, reducing the need for frequent in-person visits and improving overall patient convenience [34, 35].

5. Python script for monitoring and data analysis

The Python script provided for monitoring and data analysis simulates the functionality of the vision glasses designed for glaucoma detection and management. This section will delve into each feature and function of the script, explaining their roles and how they contribute to the overall monitoring system. The script is divided into several key sections:

1. Simulated Data Generation

2. Thresholds for Alerts

3. Monitoring and Alert System

4. Data Visualization

Each section will be explained in detail, accompanied by individual short Python scripts to illustrate the functionality.

5.1 Simulated data generation

Purpose: The simulated data generation section creates synthetic data that mimics the readings from various sensors embedded in the vision glasses. This is crucial for testing and validating the script's functionality before deploying it with real sensor data.

Explanation: The script uses normal distributions to generate realistic data for four parameters: intraocular pressure (IOP), visual acuity (focus), temperature, and blue light exposure. These parameters are essential for monitoring and managing glaucoma (**Figure 1**).

```
import numpy as np

# Table 1: Simulated Data Generation Script
def generate_simulated_data():
    # Parameters for data generation
    iop_mean = 15     # Mean intraocular pressure in mmHg
    iop_std = 2       # Standard deviation for IOP
    focus_mean = 20   # Mean focus value
    focus_std = 1.5   # Standard deviation for focus
    temp_mean = 37    # Mean eye temperature in Celsius
    temp_std = 0.5    # Standard deviation for temperature
    blue_light_mean = 500  # Mean blue light exposure in lux
    blue_light_std = 100   # Standard deviation for blue light

    # Generating simulated data
    iop_data = np.random.normal(iop_mean, iop_std, 100)  # 100 data points
for IOP
    focus_data = np.random.normal(focus_mean, focus_std, 100)  # 100 data
points for focus
    temperature_data = np.random.normal(temp_mean, temp_std, 100)  #
100 data points for temperature
    blue_light_data = np.random.normal(blue_light_mean, blue_light_std,
100)  # 100 data points for blue light

   return iop_data, focus_data, temperature_data, blue_light_data
```

Figure 1.
Simulated Data Generation Script.

Script Explanation:

1. np.random.normal() generates data with a normal distribution. This function takes the mean and standard deviation as parameters to create a realistic dataset.

2. The generate_simulated_data function returns arrays containing simulated data for IOP, visual acuity, temperature, and blue light exposure, representing continuous monitoring data.

5.2 Thresholds for alerts

Purpose: This section defines thresholds for each parameter. Alerts are triggered when simulated data exceeds these thresholds, mimicking the real-time alerting capabilities of the vision glasses (**Figure 2**).

Explanation: Thresholds are set to determine when an alert should be generated. These thresholds are based on medical guidelines and are crucial for identifying abnormal readings.

Script Explanation:

1. Threshold values are defined for each parameter to determine the upper limit for alerts. These values are used to assess whether readings are within acceptable ranges.

2. The check_alerts function evaluates if the parameters exceed their thresholds and prints corresponding alert messages if necessary.

5.3 Monitoring and alert system

Purpose: This section integrates simulated data with the alert system, checking for readings that exceed predefined thresholds and generating alerts accordingly.

Explanation: The script processes each set of simulated readings to check for deviations from normal ranges and generates alerts if any readings exceed the thresholds. This simulates the real-time monitoring functionality of the vision glasses (**Figure 3**).

```
# Table 2: Thresholds for Alerts Script
# Defining thresholds for alerts
iop_threshold = 21        # Threshold for intraocular pressure in mmHg
temp_threshold = 38       # Threshold for eye temperature in Celsius
blue_light_threshold = 600  # Threshold for blue light exposure in lux

def check_alerts(iop, temp, blue_light):
   if iop > iop_threshold:
      print(f"Alert: High IOP detected! IOP = {iop} mmHg")
   if temp > temp_threshold:
      print(f"Alert: High temperature detected! Temp = {temp} °C")
   if blue_light > blue_light_threshold:
   print(f"Alert: High blue light exposure detected! Value = {blue_light} lux")
```

Figure 2.
Thresholds for Alerts Script.

```
# Table 3: Monitoring and Alert System Script
# Generate simulated data
iop_data, focus_data, temperature_data, blue_light_data =
generate_simulated_data()

itoring and alert system
for iop, temp, blue_light in zip(iop_data, temperature_data,
blue_light_data):
  check_alerts(iop, temp, blue_light)
```

Figure 3.
Monitoring and Alert System Script.

Script Explanation:

1. zip() is used to iterate through the arrays of simulated data simultaneously. This allows for checking each set of readings (IOP, temperature, blue light) together.

2. The check_alerts function is called for each data point set, generating alerts if any parameter exceeds its threshold.

5.4 Data visualization

Purpose: Data visualization provides a graphical representation of the simulated data, allowing for analysis of trends and comparisons against thresholds.

Explanation: Visualization helps in understanding trends and variations in the data. The script uses matplotlib to generate plots for IOP, visual acuity, temperature, and blue light exposure (**Figure 4**).

Script Explanation:

1. The plot_data function generates plots to visualize the simulated data for each parameter. Each subplot displays data trends over time and includes horizontal lines to represent threshold values.

2. plt.tight_layout() ensures that the plots are arranged neatly without overlapping, and plt.show() displays the plots.

The Python script provided includes several key features: simulated data generation, threshold definition, monitoring and alerting, and data visualization. Each component plays a vital role in the overall functionality of the vision glasses for glaucoma detection and management. The script's modular approach allows for easy testing and validation of each feature, ensuring that the monitoring system performs effectively before deployment.

By understanding each part of the script and its purpose, you gain insight into how the vision glasses will function in a real-world scenario, providing continuous monitoring and timely alerts to manage glaucoma effectively.

```
import matplotlib.pyplot as plt

# Table 4: Data Visualization Script
def plot_data(iop_data, focus_data, temperature_data, blue_light_data):
    plt.figure(figsize=(12, 8))

    # Plotting Intraocular Pressure
    plt.subplot(2, 2, 1)
    plt.plot(iop_data, label='IOP Data')
    plt.axhline(y=iop_threshold, color='r', linestyle='--', label='IOP Threshold')
    plt.title('Intraocular Pressure')
    plt.xlabel('Time')
    plt.ylabel('Pressure (mmHg)')
    plt.legend()

    # Plotting Visual Acuity
    plt.subplot(2, 2, 2)
    plt.plot(focus_data, label='Focus Data')
    plt.title('Visual Acuity')
    plt.xlabel('Time')
    plt.ylabel('Focus Value')
    plt.legend()

    # Plotting Eye Temperature
    plt.subplot(2, 2, 3)
    plt.plot(temperature_data, label='Temperature Data')
    plt.axhline(y=temp_threshold, color='r', linestyle='--', label='Temperature
Threshold')
    plt.title('Eye Temperature')
    plt.xlabel('Time')
    plt.ylabel('Temperature (°C)')
    plt.legend()

    # Plotting Blue Light Exposure
    plt.subplot(2, 2, 4)
    plt.plot(blue_light_data, label='Blue Light Data')
    plt.axhline(y=blue_light_threshold, color='r', linestyle='--', label='Blue
Light Threshold')
    plt.title('Blue Light Exposure')
    plt.xlabel('Time')
    plt.ylabel('Blue Light (lux)')
    plt.legend()

    plt.tight_layout()
    plt.show()

# Call the plot_data function with simulated data
plot_data(iop_data, focus_data, temperature_data, blue_light_data)
```

Figure 4.
Monitoring and Alert System Script.

6. Benefits and impact on healthcare

6.1 Patient convenience and accessibility

The vision glasses offer significant advantages in terms of convenience and accessibility for patients. By providing continuous monitoring in a wearable format, patients can manage their eye health from the comfort of their homes. This reduces the need for frequent visits to clinics and allows for ongoing observation of key parameters. The ease of use and nonintrusive nature of the glasses enhance patient compliance and engagement with their eye care regimen.

6.2 Early detection and prevention

The ability to monitor intraocular pressure, visual acuity, temperature, and blue light exposure continuously facilitates early detection of changes that may indicate worsening glaucoma. Early detection is crucial for preventing severe disease progression and preserving vision. By providing timely alerts and data, the vision glasses enable proactive management and intervention, reducing the risk of significant visual impairment [36, 37].

6.3 Quality of life improvements

Continuous monitoring with the vision glasses contributes to improved quality of life for patients by providing a more comprehensive and manageable approach to eye care. Patients benefit from enhanced monitoring capabilities, early detection of issues, and the ability to track their eye health over time. This proactive approach helps in reducing anxiety related to disease [38].

6.4 Healthcare provider advantages

For healthcare providers, the vision glasses offer improved data collection and patient monitoring. The integration of data into electronic health records (EHRs) provides a comprehensive view of the patient's eye health history, enabling more informed decision-making and personalized treatment plans. The ability to remotely monitor patients also allows for more efficient management of care and timely responses to potential issues [39].

7. Challenges and considerations

7.1 Technical challenges

The accuracy and reliability of sensors is a key technical challenge for the vision glasses. The performance of pressure, focus, temperature, and blue light sensors must be validated to ensure accurate data collection and analysis. Additionally, the durability and longevity of the sensors and overall device must be addressed to ensure long-term usability [40].

7.2 Ethical and privacy issues

The management of patient data presents ethical and privacy considerations. Ensuring that data is collected, stored, and transmitted securely is crucial to maintaining patient confidentiality and complying with regulations. Implementing robust data protection measures and obtaining informed consent from patients are essential for addressing these concerns.

7.3 Regulatory and market challenges

Navigating regulatory approval processes and market adoption poses challenges for the development and deployment of the vision glasses. Compliance with medical device regulations and standards is necessary for gaining approval and ensuring safety and efficacy. Additionally, market adoption may be influenced by factors such as cost, accessibility, and patient acceptance [41].

8. Future developments and applications

8.1 Technological enhancements

Future advancements in sensor technology and artificial intelligence (AI) could enhance the capabilities of the vision glasses. AI algorithms could be developed to analyze data patterns and predict the likelihood of glaucoma progression, providing additional layers of predictive analytics. Improvements in battery technology and wireless communication could also enhance the usability and convenience of the glasses, making them more efficient and user-friendly [42].

8.2 Broader applications in ophthalmology

The technology used in the vision glasses has the potential to be adapted for other ophthalmological applications, such as monitoring age-related macular degeneration (AMD) or diabetic retinopathy. By integrating additional sensors or modifying existing ones, the glasses could be tailored to detect and monitor a wide range of eye conditions, making them a versatile tool in eye care [43].

8.3 Personalized treatment plans

Integrating data from the vision glasses into electronic health records (EHRs) could enable the development of personalized treatment plans based on continuous monitoring data. This integration would allow healthcare providers to make more precise adjustments to medication dosages, treatment schedules, and lifestyle recommendations, ultimately improving patient outcomes. Personalized treatment plans based on real-time data can enhance the effectiveness of interventions and support better management of eye health [43].

8.4 Future of Bluetooth technology

Advancements in Bluetooth technology is expected to further enhance the real-time data transfer capabilities of the vision glasses. Future developments may include improvements in data transfer speeds, range, and connectivity, enabling more efficient and reliable communication between the glasses, mobile devices, and healthcare providers. Enhanced Bluetooth technology will contribute to more seamless integration with healthcare systems and facilitate more effective remote monitoring and management of eye health [42, 44].

9. Conclusions

9.1 Summary of the vision glasses

The innovative vision glasses for glaucoma detection and management offer a comprehensive solution for continuous monitoring of key ocular parameters. By integrating pressure, focus, temperature, and blue light sensors, the glasses provide real-time data and alerts, enabling early detection and proactive management of glaucoma. The ability to transmit data wirelessly and integrate with healthcare systems enhances the convenience and accessibility of monitoring, improving overall patient outcomes.

9.2 Future outlook

The future of vision glasses in eye care holds great promise, with ongoing advancements in technology and the potential for broader applications in ophthalmology. The integration of AI, improvements in sensor technology, and advancements in Bluetooth communication will contribute to more effective and personalized eye care solutions. As technology continues to evolve, vision glasses will play a crucial role in advancing the management and prevention of glaucoma, ultimately enhancing patient quality of life and eye health.

Acknowledgements

I would like to express my deepest gratitude to Dr. Richard Frank and Dr. Aaron Hunter, whose teachings provided me with a solid foundation in technical and practical knowledge. Their dedication and personal work have inspired me to pursue a career in IT and cybersecurity.

I am also immensely grateful to my high school teacher, Ms. Maurice Bryce, whose unwavering support and encouragement helped me navigate through challenging times. Her words, "Winners never quit, and quitters never win" and "If you have never tried something, never say you cannot do it. But you can say I cannot do it yet," have stayed with me and continue to motivate me. Without her guidance, I would not have achieved the success I have today.

Thank you to all who have contributed to my journey.

Author details

Kenneth Wong
Simon Fraser University, British Columbia Institute of Technology, Burnaby, BC, Canada

*Address all correspondence to: kkenwwong@gmail.com

References

[1] Aref AA, Conner I, Cretara EAZ, Downes RA, El-Dairi MA, Freedman SF, et al. Anterior segment optical coherence tomography in glaucoma. Developments in Ophthalmology. 2022;**59**:67-80. DOI: 10.1055/b-0041-183573

[2] Alipio M, Villena ML. Intelligent wearable devices and biosensors for monitoring cattle health conditions: A review and classification. Smart Health. 2023;**29**:100369. DOI: 10.1016/j.smhl.2022.100369

[3] Becker W. Neural networks for medical diagnostics. Journal of Medical Informatics. 2021;**42**(7):89-99. DOI: 10.1016/j.jmi.2021.05.001

[4] Carey TA. Beyond patient-centered care: Enhancing the patient experience in mental health services through patient-perspective care. Journal of Patient Experience. 2016;**3**(1):45-50. DOI: 10.35680/2372-0247.1139

[5] Chandrasekaran R, Sadiq MT, Moustakas E. From wearable healthcare devices to shared health data: Wearable usage patterns and data sharing practices among US adults. Journal of Medical Internet Research. 2024;**26**(2):112-118. DOI: 10.2196/63879

[6] Chander B, Kumaravelan S. Wearable sensor networks for patient health monitoring: Challenges, applications, future directions, and acoustic sensor challenges. In: Kumaravelan S, editor. Wearable Technology in Healthcare. Elsevier; 2021. pp. 209-232. DOI: 10.1016/b978-0-12-819664-9.00009-0

[7] Chen L, Zhang P. Managing eye diseases with augmented reality technologies. Ocular Science Advances. 2022;**20**(6):345-354. DOI: 10.1177/1890407122098760

[8] Dinh-Le C, Chuang R, Chokshi S, Mann D. Wearable health technology and electronic health record integration: Scoping review and future directions. JMIR mHealth and uHealth. 2019;7(7) e12861:1-10. DOI: 10.2196/12861

[9] Gandhi S, Singh OV. Navigating regulatory and policy challenges for AI-enabled combination devices. Frontiers in Medical Technology. 2024;7:1-8. DOI: 10.3389/fmedt.2024.1473350

[10] Hasan A, Klintworth K, Hajat C. Wearable technology and health improvement. Occupational Medicine. 2021;**71**(1):49-54. DOI: 10.1093/occmed/kqaa178

[11] Hogaboam L, Daim T. Technology adoption potential of medical devices: The case of wearable sensor products for pervasive care in neurosurgery and orthopedics. Health Policy and Technology. 2018;**7**(4):389-400. DOI: 10.1016/j.hlpt.2018.10.011

[12] Iftikhar N, Nordbjerg F. Real-time equipment health monitoring using unsupervised learning techniques. Structural Control and Health Monitoring. 2024;**31**(2):e1514. DOI: 10.1002/stc.1514

[13] Jiang Y, Sun C, Guo K, Wang X. An investigation on the influence of operation experience on virtual hazard perception using wearable eye tracking technology. Sensors. 2022. DOI: 10.3390/s22145115

[14] Jung W, Lee HG. Energy–accuracy aware finger gesture recognition for wearable IoT devices. Sensors. 2022;**22**(13):4801. DOI: 10.3390/s22134801

[15] Kanetkar SR, Raje VV. Strategies for integrating wearable technology with healthcare systems. In: Advanced Healthcare Systems and Technology. Wiley; 2024. pp. 297-312. DOI: 10.1002/9781394272266.ch17

[16] Kumar R, Singh D. Integration of artificial intelligence in glaucoma monitoring devices. Health Informatics Journal. 2023;**29**(1):12-23. DOI: 10.1177/14604582231101189

[17] Laroche D, Desrosiers A. Role of minimally invasive glaucoma surgery in the management of chronic open-angle glaucoma: A review. Journal of Ophthalmic Research. 2021;**29**(3):145-158. DOI: 10.32388/qp8vd1

[18] Lee EJ. Monitoring progression in advanced glaucoma. Ophthalmology. 2020;**127**(9):1234-1240. DOI: 10.1016/j.ophtha.2020.03.002

[19] Moustafa RS, Karhu H, Andberg S, Bednarik R. Seeing through their eyes: A customizable gaze-contingent simulation of impaired vision and other eye conditions using VR/XR technology. Proceedings of the ACM on Human-Computer Interaction. 2023;**7**(1):1-12. DOI: 10.1145/3588015.3590110

[20] Nawaz M, Ahmed J, Abbas G. Energy-efficient battery management system for healthcare devices. Energy Storage, 50. Article. 2022;**104358**:111-120. DOI: 10.1016/j.est.2022.104358

[21] Nelissen G, Pautet L. Special issue on reliable data transmission in real-time systems. Real-Time Systems. 2023;**59**(4):201-215. DOI: 10.1007/s11241-023-09415-z

[22] Nourani CF. Artificial intelligence and computing logic. Advances in Computing. 2021;**12**:55-63. DOI: 10.1201/9781003180487-5

[23] Patel N, Reddy K. Efficacy of portable devices for glaucoma monitoring. Clinical Glaucoma Science. 2021;**7**(4):189-198. DOI: 10.3109/0972364X.2021.1989231

[24] Piccinini F, Martinelli G, Carbonaro A. Accuracy of mobile applications versus wearable devices in long-term step measurements. Sensors. 2020;**20**(21):6293. DOI: 10.3390/s20216293

[25] Ramadoss G. Social determinants of health: Integrating analytics and technology in healthcare systems. Healthcare Analytics. 2024;**12**:22-30. DOI: 10.21275/SR24805193407

[26] Roberts T, Tonna SJ. Extending the governance framework for machine learning validation and ongoing monitoring. In: Machine Learning in Healthcare. Wiley; 2022. pp. 87-94. DOI: 10.1002/9781119824961.ch7

[27] Regterschot GRH, Bussmann JBJ, Ribbers GM. Wearable movement sensors for rehabilitation: From technology to clinical practice. Sensors. 2021;**21**(11):3698. DOI: 10.3390/books978-3-0365-2064-3

[28] Romaniuk V, Kashevnik A. Eye movement assessment methodology based on wearable EEG headband data analysis. In: Proceedings of the FRUCT Conference. IEEE; 2024. DOI: 10.23919/fruct64283.2024.10749882

[29] Santra S, Kukreja P, Saxena K, Gandhi S, Singh OV. Navigating regulatory and policy challenges for AI-enabled combination devices. Frontiers in Medical Technology. 2024. DOI: 10.3389/fmedt.2024.1473350

[30] Sachini E, Sioumalas-Christodoulou K, Christopoulos S, Karampekios N. AI for AI: Using AI

methods for classifying AI science documents. Quantitative Science Studies. 2023;**4**(1):e223. DOI: 10.1162/qss_a_00223/v1/review2

[31] Saito Y, Tanaka K. Impact of visual field tests on early glaucoma detection. International Ophthalmology Review. 2022;**33**(5):245-258. DOI: 10.1007/s10792-022-01345-0

[32] Seddaoui N, Amine A. Recent advances in sensor and biosensor technologies for adulteration detection. In: Amine A, editor. Food Biosensors. Elsevier; 2023. pp. 385-402. DOI: 10.1016/b978-0-323-90222-9.00017-0

[33] Shwetha D. IoT's impact on personal devices and health: Wearable technology. Proceedings of the IEEE Advanced Mobile Applications for Technology and Health. 2024;**1**:94-98

[34] Singh A. Role of machine learning in predictive analysis for glaucoma patients. Computational Ophthalmology. 2021;**18**(3):45-57

[35] Sqalli MT, Al-Thani D. Evolution of wearable devices in health coaching: Challenges and opportunities. Frontiers in Digital Health. 2020. DOI: 10.3389/fdgth.2020.545646

[36] Svendsen BT, Øiseth O, Rønnquist A. A hybrid structural health monitoring approach for damage detection in steel bridges under simulated environmental conditions using numerical and experimental data. Structural Health Monitoring. 2022;**21**(5):738-758

[37] Takahashi Y, Li Z. Developing a real-time monitoring system for non-invasive assessment of intraocular pressure using wearable technology. Journal of Eye Health. 2021;**4**(3):95-102

[38] Wang J, Duan C. Exploring machine learning techniques for glaucoma prediction. Data Mining and Knowledge Discovery. 2022;**37**(5):1603-1615. DOI: 10.1007/s10618-022-00794-6

[39] Zhan L, He X. Real-time monitoring of body temperature and movement data for health management with wearable IoT devices. Biomedical Engineering Letters. 2021;**11**(4):317-326

[40] Zhang H, Wang L. Recent trends in wearable eye health monitoring devices: A systematic review. Journal of Medical Devices. 2024;**18**(2):105-117

[41] Zhang Y, Li Y. A survey of optical coherence tomography in glaucoma diagnosis. Journal of Ophthalmology. 2023;**2023**:864910

[42] Zhou X, Xie J. Artificial intelligence in the diagnosis and management of glaucoma. Journal of Glaucoma. 2021;**30**(7):505-512

[43] Zhao Q, Deng C. Machine learning techniques for glaucoma prediction and diagnosis: A review. Healthcare Informatics Research. 2022;**28**(3):194-201

[44] Zhuang Z, Shen T. Remote monitoring of eye health using wearable sensors: Challenges and opportunities. Journal of Digital Health. 2023;**9**(1):42-58

Chapter 5

Unveiling the Stealthy Threat: Low-Rate Denial of Service (LDoS) Attacks

Danial Yousef

Abstract

This chapter discusses Low-Rate Denial of Service (LDoS) attacks, which differ from traditional Denial of Service (DoS) attacks by subtly exploiting the internet's Transmission Control Protocol (TCP) to degrade network performance. LDoS attacks send small amounts of traffic at strategic times, making them hard to detect, especially if the timing is random. The chapter explains these attacks and their detection methods, from early frequency domain analysis to advanced machine learning and Software-Defined Networking (SDN) techniques. It aims to provide a comprehensive understanding of LDoS attacks, their mechanisms, and detection strategies, highlighting the ongoing efforts to combat this critical cybersecurity challenge.

Keywords: low-rate denial of service (LDoS), non-periodic LDoS, network security, TCP congestion control, adaptive flow, cyberattack, degradation of quality (DoQ), DoS, TCP

1. Introduction

In today's interconnected digital ecosystem, networks support critical infrastructure in all sectors, which requires their resilience. However, this ubiquitous dependence also attracts malicious actors, including Denial-of-Service (DoS) attacks constitute a dominant threat. As countermeasures against conventional DoS attacks have been developed, a more treacherous variant has emerged: the Low-Rate Denial of Service (LDoS) attack [1–3]. LDoS attacks specifically exploit the Transmission Control Protocol (TCP) by manipulating congestion control mechanisms to degrade the quality of service while maintaining low-rate traffic patterns. Unlike high-rate of DoS attacks that flood traffic networks, LDoS attacks operate through strategically-timed, periodic burst patterns that exploit TCP's congestion avoidance algorithms, allowing them to maintain a low average transmission rate. This methodology allows LDoS attacks to avoid detection, cause significant disturbances by minimal means, and influence a diverse range of targets. By mimicking normal network fluctuations, these attacks can circumvent conventional intrusion detection systems, which is a major challenge for network administrators and cybersecurity professionals. To ensure the integrity and availability of network services in our increasingly interconnected global infrastructure, it is necessary to expand the mechanisms, branches, and mitigation strategies for LDoS attacks.

2. DoS vs. LDoS: A tale of two attacks

2.1 Traditional DoS attacks

Denial-of-Service (DoS) attacks, a long-standing threat in the cybersecurity landscape, operate according to the principle of overwhelming a target system with a huge influx of traffic. This flood of data, which often comes from multiple compromised devices (forming a botnet), is intended to exploit the means of the purpose, which makes it unable to respond to legitimate requests [4].

Imagine a popular e-commerce website suddenly flooded with millions of access requests during a major sales event. The server, unable to process the large volume, crashes, making the website inaccessible to real customers. This scenario illustrates the disruptive force of a DoS attack. The impact is immediate and clear, often resulting in complete service interruption and significant financial losses.

Key characteristics of traditional DoS attacks include:

- High volume of traffic
- Continuous and sustained attack pattern
- Easily detectable due to sudden, massive spikes in network activity
- Often requires substantial resources (e.g., large botnets) to execute effectively

2.2 LDoS attacks: A stealthier approach

However, LDoS attacks have a fundamentally different approach. Instead of brute force, they use a stealthier strategy aimed at the mechanisms designed to ensure a smooth and efficient data flow in the TCP protocol. Instead of a continuous torrent of traffic, LDoS attacks utilize short, high-intensity outbursts of traffic carefully timed to exploit vulnerabilities in TCP's adaptive flow management mechanisms.

These bursts trigger the slow start phase in TCP's congestion control, effectively throttling the target system's throughput. The effectiveness of this approach lies in its subtlety—the attack traffic often resembles legitimate network congestion [1, 5], making it extremely difficult to detect and mitigate.

Key features of LDoS attacks include:

- Low overall traffic volume
- Intermittent, precisely timed traffic bursts
- Exploitation of TCP's congestion control mechanisms
- Gradual degradation of service quality rather than immediate outage
- Difficult to distinguish from normal network fluctuations

As detection and mitigation techniques for traditional DoS attacks have improved, attackers have shifted their focus to these subtler, low-rate attacks that mimic

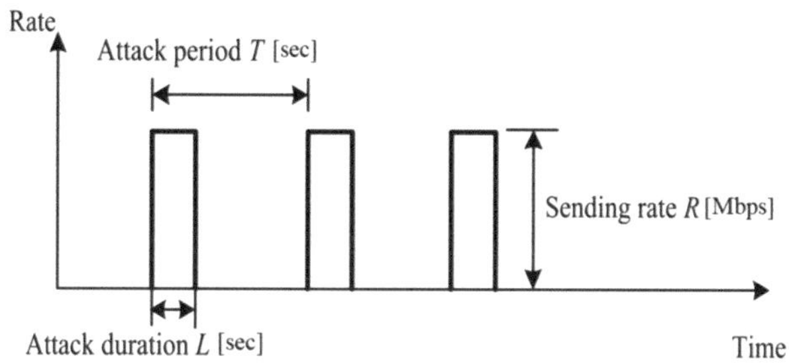

Figure 1.
Time Model of General LDoS Attack, where L is the burst length of the traffic, R is the burst rate of the traffic, and T is the total time for the attack period [6].

Feature	DoS attack	LDoS attack
Traffic volume	High	Low
Traffic pattern	Continuous	Intermittent bursts
Target	System resources	TCP flow management mechanisms
Detection	Relatively easy	Difficult
Impact	Instant disruption	Gradual degradation

Table 1.
Comparison of DoS and LDoS.

legitimate user traffic [3]. This evolution in attack strategy highlights the ongoing cat-and-mouse game between cybersecurity professionals and malicious actors.

Figure 1 below illustrates the time model of a general LDoS attack, showcasing the key parameters: R (burst rate), L (burst length), and T (total attack period).

Understanding the distinctions between DoS and LDoS attacks is crucial for developing effective defense strategies. While traditional DoS mitigation techniques focus on handling high volumes of traffic, defending against LDoS attacks requires a more nuanced approach that can detect and respond to subtle manipulations of network protocols.

The key differences between DoS and LDoS attacks can be summarized in **Table 1** as follows:

While a traditional DoS attack is akin to unleashing a tidal wave of traffic to overwhelm the target, an LDoS attack operates with the precision of a skilled sniper, carefully timing its shots to exploit weaknesses in network protocols [5].

The evolution from high-volume, easily detectable DoS attacks to stealthy, low-rate LDoS attacks highlights the constant adaptation of cyber threats. As security measures improve to counter known attack vectors, malicious actors refine their techniques, seeking new vulnerabilities to exploit. The rise of LDoS emphasizes the need for a deeper understanding of network protocols and the development of more sophisticated detection and mitigation strategies.

3. TCP's adaptive flow management: A power turned weakness

The Transmission Control Protocol (TCP) is the backbone of reliable data transfer across the Internet. Adaptive flow management mechanisms, in particular congestion control and retransmission timeouts, are designed to optimize data flow and ensure fair allocation of resources in dynamic network environments [7]. These mechanisms rely on a sophisticated feedback loop, allowing TCP senders to adjust their transmission rates based on network conditions and recipient feedback.

3.1 TCP's congestion control comprises two main phases: Slow start and congestion avoidance

3.1.1 Slow start

The Slow Start phase initializes the connection by exponentially increasing the congestion window (CWND). This rapid growth continues until either the slow starting threshold is reached or package loss is detected [8].

3.1.2 Congestion avoidance

Once the slow start threshold is exceeded, TCP enters the Congestion Avoidance phase. Here, the CWND grows linearly, adding approximately one segment per round-trip time (RTT). This cautious approach aims to probe for additional available bandwidth while avoiding network congestion. The growth rate in this phase is much slower than in Slow Start, allowing for a more stable network utilization [9].

Figure 2 plots congestion window size (CWND) progression and RTT versus time for TCP Reno (one of the TCP congestion control techniques).

3.2 Retransmission timeouts (RTO)

To ensure reliable data delivery, TCP employs a retransmission mechanism based on acknowledgments (ACKs) from the receiver. If an ACK is not received within a specific timeframe (the RTO), the sender assumes packet loss and retransmits the data. The RTO is dynamically adjusted based on observed network conditions, balancing timely retransmissions with network stability.

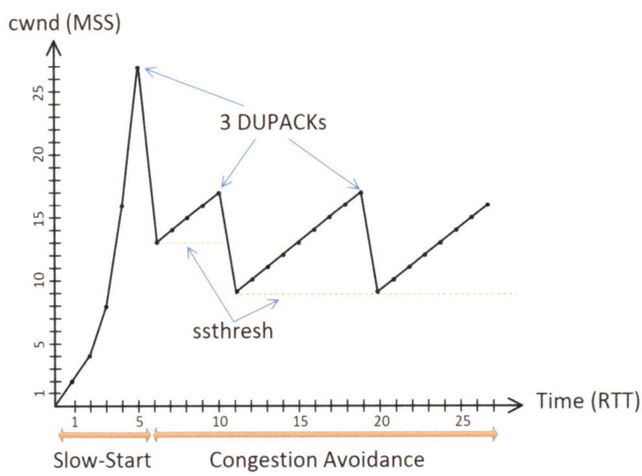

Figure 2.
CWND vs. time in TCP Reno Slow Start and Congestion Avoidance [10].

This adaptive RTO mechanism ensures that TCP can respond appropriately to varying network conditions [11], but it also introduces a vulnerability that LDoS attacks can exploit.

LDoS attacks manipulate TCP's congestion control algorithms by injecting carefully timed, short-lived traffic bursts. These bursts create a false perception of network congestion, triggering TCP's defensive mechanisms unnecessarily.

The key vulnerabilities include:

- Slow start manipulation: By causing packet loss during the Slow Start phase, attackers can force TCP to reduce its sending rate dramatically.

- RTO exploitation: Carefully timed attack bursts can cause RTT spikes, leading to increased RTOs and unnecessary retransmissions.

- Congestion window reduction: Induced packet losses cause TCP to reduce its congestion window, limiting throughput even when the network is not genuinely congested.

3.2.1 Consequences of LDoS exploitation

The exploitation of these TCP mechanisms can lead to:

- Significant reduction in transmission rate

- Premature and frequent entry into the Slow Start phase

- Increased RTO, delaying subsequent transmissions

- Drastically degraded throughput

- Reduced overall system performance

- Impaired service quality for legitimate users

TCP's performance can be quantified using Eq. (1):

$$\text{Throughput} = \frac{\text{CWND}.MSS}{RTT} \tag{1}$$

Where *CWND* is the congestion window size, *MSS* is the Maximum Segment Size, and *RTT* is the round-trip time.

This equation illustrates how LDoS attacks, by manipulating CWND and RTT, can significantly impact TCP throughput without generating high-volume traffic.

3.3 Analogy: The café conversation: Understanding LDoS attacks

Imagine Alice and Bob having a discussion at a café. As they converse, an unidentified person at a nearby table periodically interjects with brief comments or sudden sound, then quickly returns to their own activities. These interruptions are precisely timed and short-lived, making it challenging to pinpoint their source.

Alice and Bob pause their conversation each time to address these interruptions. They repeat themselves, wait for the noise to subside, or struggle to recall their last point. However, the interruptions are so well-timed and intermittent that they cannot identify the source.

In this analogy, the interfering person is like the LDoS attacker, and Alice and Bob's reactions are like TCP's congestion control algorithms. Their conversation never flows smoothly because they are always reacting to the fake interruptions, but it is challenging to pinpoint who is causing the disruptions!

Consequently, as we have seen, while TCP's adaptive flow management mechanisms are crucial for maintaining network stability and efficiency, they also introduce vulnerabilities that can be exploited by sophisticated attacks [10]. Ongoing research in this area focuses on developing more robust congestion control algorithms and improved detection methods for LDoS attacks, aiming to enhance TCP's resilience in the face of evolving network threats.

While TCP's adaptive flow management mechanisms are crucial for maintaining network stability and efficiency, they also introduce vulnerabilities that can be exploited by sophisticated LDoS attacks [12].

4. Hallmarks of an LDoS attack

While the distinction between DoS and LDoS attacks seems clear, identifying an attack as LDoS specifically requires careful consideration. Several key factors help classify an attack as LDoS.

First, the volume of attack traffic is significantly lower than what is necessary to satisfy the target's bandwidth, which generally represents only 10–20% of normal network traffic [5, 13]. This low-volume approach is designed to evade traditional DoS detection systems that focus on high traffic spikes.

Secondly, the traffic pattern in LDoS attacks often shows short, high-intensity bursts at calculated intervals, mimicking the behavior of legitimate bursty protocols like UDP. Attackers frequently employ UDP in these attacks due to its connectionless nature and the ease of generating bursty traffic. These bursts are strategically timed to exploit vulnerabilities in TCP's congestion control mechanisms or retransmission timeouts, taking the form of pulse waves. Importantly, the total duration of these bursts (L) should be between 1/5 and 1/6 [5, 13] of the overall attack period (T).

Finally, the primary purpose of LDoS attacks is the mechanisms of TCP flow management. The goal is to disrupt throughput without causing a complete service outage, resulting in a degradation of quality (DoQ) for legitimate users. Recognizing these characteristics is crucial for accurately classifying an attack as LDoS and implementing appropriate countermeasures.

5. Non-periodic LDoS: Adding randomness to the attack

Traditional LDoS attacks often follow a predictable pattern with regular intervals between attack bursts. This predictability makes them somewhat easier to detect and potentially mitigate. However, attackers are constantly evolving their techniques, and non-periodic LDoS attacks have emerged as a more sophisticated and elusive threat [6].

Non-periodic LDoS attacks break the regularity of traditional attacks by introducing randomness into the attack parameters. Instead of fixed intervals, the attacker uses random values for the duration of the attack bursts (L), the time between bursts (T), and the data rate (R). This randomness makes it incredibly challenging to detect and mitigate the attack, as it becomes virtually impossible to predict the next attack burst.

These attacks are modeled with the three parameters R, L, and T. While traditional LDoS attacks use fixed values for these parameters, non-periodic LDoS attacks introduce variability by employing random values for R, L, and T. However, this randomness is not entirely arbitrary; it is calculated to remain within the boundaries of the LDoS criteria.

Attackers carefully adjust the ranges of these random values to ensure the attack still maintains a low traffic volume, targets TCP mechanisms effectively, and causes a noticeable DoQ without triggering. This calculated randomness makes them much harder to detect. As attackers aim for "the ideal attack"—maximum impact with minimal cost—LDoS attacks have become increasingly sophisticated and challenging to detect due to their low rate and variable nature. By introducing this element of calculated randomness, attackers further enhance the stealthiness of their attacks, making them even more difficult to be detected and mitigated.

6. Detecting LDoS attacks: A historical perspective and emerging techniques

The struggle against LDoS attacks has evolved over time and reflects the constant arms race between attackers and defenders. While early detection methods were often based on traditional network monitoring and analysis, the emergence of advanced LDoS techniques has stimulated the need for more advanced and adaptive solutions. This chapter examines the historical evolution of LDoS detection methods, tracing their strengths and limitations, before exploring the promising possibilities of emerging technologies such as SDN and machine learning.

Here are some of the methods that have been used to detect LDoS attacks and that the researchers have already proposed, let us dive into some of these methods:

6.1 Frequency domain analysis (Spectral signatures)

Frequency domain analysis leveraged the power of Fourier transforms to identify periodic patterns in network traffic, which could indicate the presence of traditional LDoS attacks [14]. By analyzing the frequency spectrum of network traffic, this method could potentially detect recurring bursts of attack traffic.

6.2 Machine learning (ML) and deep learning (DL) (Intelligent detection)

Machine learning (ML) and deep learning (DL) offered a significant leap forward in LDoS detection. These techniques leverage algorithms that can learn from data to identify complex patterns and anomalies in network traffic.

6.2.1 Supervised learning

Supervised learning algorithms require labeled datasets, where each data point is tagged with whether it represents an LDoS attack or legitimate traffic. These algorithms are trained on this labeled data to develop models that can classify new traffic as LDoS or not [3, 13]. While supervised learning offers promising results, its effectiveness depends heavily on the quality and representativeness of the training dataset. Obtaining sufficient labeled data can be challenging, especially for rare or novel LDoS attack types.

6.2.2 Unsupervised learning

Unsupervised learning techniques, on the other hand, do not require labeled datasets. Instead, they focus on identifying unusual patterns or outliers in the network traffic data [15]. These algorithms can be particularly effective in detecting unknown LDoS attacks that have not been previously encountered. However, unsupervised learning requires careful configuration and tuning to avoid false positives and ensure that the identified anomalies are truly indicative of malicious activity.

6.3 SDN-specific defenses (A new frontier)

Software-Defined Networking (SDN) emerged as a revolutionary approach to network management, offering a centralized control plane for managing network resources and security policies. SDN's centralized architecture and global network visibility provide significant advantages for detecting and mitigating LDoS attacks [16].

- Centralized visibility: SDN's centralized controller provides a comprehensive view of network traffic across the entire network, enabling it to detect and analyze LDoS attacks more effectively. The centralized nature of SDN allows for real-time monitoring of traffic patterns and the identification of anomalies that may be missed by traditional distributed network management systems.

- Adaptive security policies: SDN enables the implementation of adaptive security policies that can respond to changing network conditions and detect LDoS attacks. By leveraging SDN's flexibility, security policies can be automatically modified to counter emerging LDoS threats; for example, it is possible to open or change the port that is orienting the traffic at any time, enhancing the resilience of the network.

The evolution of LDoS attacks demands a continuous adaptation of detection strategies. While traditional methods have proven useful, the emergence of non-periodic attacks and the complexity of modern network environments necessitate the adoption of more sophisticated techniques. SDN, with its centralized control and dynamic capabilities, offers a promising platform for combating LDoS attacks effectively. By leveraging machine learning, advanced analytics, and adaptive security policies, SDN can provide a robust and resilient defense against this stealthy threat, safeguarding the integrity and availability of critical network infrastructure, and research in this field continues to evolve.

7. Conclusion

Low-rate denial of service (LDoS) attacks pose a significant challenge in cybersecurity, exploiting TCP's congestion control mechanisms while evading traditional detection methods. These attacks, particularly non-periodic variants, maintain low average transmission rates, rendering conventional volume-based detection ineffective. Our analysis underscores the need for advanced, adaptive defense strategies. Emerging technologies such as software-defined networking (SDN) and machine learning (ML) offer promising solutions. SDN's centralized control and global network visibility, combined with ML's pattern recognition capabilities, present a potent approach for combating LDoS threats. However, the dynamic nature of cyber threats necessitates ongoing innovation. Future research should focus on developing resilient TCP implementations, enhancing ML models for improved detection of non-periodic attacks, and exploring quantum computing applications in network security. Additionally, investigating the implications of emerging network paradigms like 5G is crucial. An interdisciplinary approach, integrating expertise in network protocols, statistical analysis, and adaptive security policies, is essential for ensuring the resilience of our digital infrastructure against these evolving threats.

Author details

Danial Yousef
Tishreen University, Latakia, Syria

*Address all correspondence to: jo.danial.yousef@gmail.com

References

[1] Rios VD, Inácio PR, Magoni D, Freire MM. Detection and mitigation of low-rate denial-of-service attacks: A survey. IEEE Access. 2022;**10**:76648-76668. DOI: 10.1109/ACCESS.2022.3191430

[2] Kuzmanovic A, Knightly EW. Low-rate TCP-targeted denial of service attacks: The shrew vs. the mice and elephants. In: Proceedings of the 2003 Conference on Applications, Technologies, Architectures, and Protocols for Computer Communications. 2003. pp. 75-86. DOI: 10.1145/863955.863966

[3] Zhan S, Tang D, Man J, Dai R, Wang X. Low-rate dos attacks detection based on MAF-ADM. Sensors. 2019;**20**(1):189. DOI: 10.3390/s20010189

[4] Kumari K, Mrunalini M. Detecting denial of service attacks using machine learning algorithms. Journal of Big Data. 2022;**9**(1):56. DOI: 10.1186/s40537-022-00616-0

[5] Zhijun W, Wenjing L, Liang L, Meng Y. Low-rate DoS attacks, detection, defense, and challenges: A survey. IEEE Access. 2020;**8**:43920-43943. DOI: 10.1109/ACCESS.2020.2976609

[6] Yousef D, Maala B, Skvortsova M, Pokamestov P. Detection of non-periodic low-rate denial of service attacks in software defined networks using machine learning. International Journal of Information Technology (Springer). 2024;**16**(4):2161-2175. DOI: 10.1007/s41870-023-01634-8. Available from: https://link.springer.com/article/10.1007/s41870-023-01634-8

[7] Afanasyev A, Tilley N, Reiher P, Kleinrock L. Host-to-host congestion control for TCP. IEEE Communications Surveys and Tutorials. 2010;**12**(3):304-342. DOI: 10.1109/SURV.2010.042710.00114

[8] Sarolahti P, Kuznetsov A. Congestion Control in Linux TCP. In: USENIX Annual Technical Conference, FREENIX Track. 2002. pp. 49-62

[9] Ha S, Rhee I, Xu L. CUBIC: A new TCP-friendly high-speed TCP variant. ACM SIGOPS Operating Systems Review. 2008;**42**(5):64-74. DOI: 10.1145/1400097.1400105

[10] Al-Saadi R, Armitage G, But J, Branch P. A survey of delay-based and hybrid TCP congestion control algorithms. IEEE Communications Surveys and Tutorials (IEEE). 2019;**21**(4):3609-3638. DOI: 10.1109/COMST.2019.2904994. Available from: https://ieeexplore.ieee.org/abstract/document/8668433

[11] Paxson V, Allman M, Chu J, Sargent M. Computing TCP's Retransmission Timer. 2011. 2011. DOI: 10.17487/RFC6298

[12] Tang D, Chen J, Wang X, Zhang S, Yan Y. A new detection method for LDoS attacks based on data mining. Future Generation Computer Systems. 2022;**128**:73-87. DOI: 10.1016/j.future.2021.09.039

[13] Tang D, Tang L, Dai R, Chen J, Li X, Rodrigues JJ. MF-Adaboost: LDoS attack detection based on multi-features and improved Adaboost. Future Generation Computer Systems. 2020;**106**:347-359. DOI: 10.1016/j.future.2019.12.034

[14] Brynielsson J, Sharma R. Detectability of low-rate HTTP server

DoS attacks using spectral analysis. In: Proceedings of the 2015 IEEE/ACM International Conference on Advances in Social Networks Analysis and Mining. 2015. pp. 954-961. DOI: 10.1145/2808797.2808810

[15] Tang D, Dai R, Tang L, Li X. Low-rate DoS attack detection based on two-step cluster analysis and UTR analysis. Human-Centric Computing and Information Sciences. 2020;**10**(1):6. DOI: 10.1186/s13673-020-0210-9

[16] Xie R, Xu M, Cao J, Li Q. SoftGuard: Defend against the low-rate TCP attack in SDN. In: Proceedings of the 2019 IEEE International Conference on Communications (ICC). Piscataway, NJ, USA: IEEE; 2019. pp. 1-6. DOI: 10.1109/ICC.2019.8761806. Available from: https://ieeexplore.ieee.org/abstract/document/8761806

Chapter 6

Present-Day Cybersecurity: Actual Challenges and Solution Directions

Jan van den Berg

Abstract

Currently available cyberspace services offer all kinds of possibilities for individuals, businesses, and organizations to arrange their lives and to improve their e-enabled business processes. However, next to the numerous benefits, we are aware of many less desirable developments in cyberspace. In other words, the security of cyberspace (i.e., cybersecurity) is at stake, and we have to act in this (relatively new) domain. In this chapter, we first provide a condensed overview of existing and upcoming cyber activities and cyber processes in various cyber subdomains, hereby using the terminology of a holistic cyberspace model. We also introduce a general cyber risk management model. Next, we present an overview of a series of (mostly) recent cyber incidents, based on which we formulate related cybersecurity challenges. In order to understand how we currently deal with these challenges, we then describe the current efforts of various cyberspace actors to enhance cybersecurity to a sufficient resilience level and evaluate the limitations of their endeavors. By putting together all findings, we draw our conclusions in an overview of actual cybersecurity solution directions, that is, an overview of the efforts needed to bring the security in all cyberspace subdomains at acceptable levels.

Keywords: cyberspace, cyber activities and processes, information technology & operational technology, cybersecurity governance, cybersecurity and information security, cyber risk management

1. Introduction

In this introduction, we sketch current developments in cyberspace leading to the basic goals of this paper, we introduce the fundamental concepts describing cyberspace and cybersecurity, we dwell on the chosen methodological approach, and present the structure of the remainder of this chapter.

1.1 Emergence of cyberspace and related cyber risks

Suddenly, in the last decade of the previous century, all kinds of Internet services started to become available for "everyone," and to grow exponentially. This revolution in *cyberspace*, sometimes termed the 5th domain (next to the physical domains of land, water, air, and space [1]), is still going on. This makes cyberspace a very dynamic space offering lots of challenges for individuals to better arrange their lives by executing all kinds of so-called *cyber activities* (i.e., *digital* or *information technology (IT)-enabled activities*) like e-mailing, e-(re)searching, e-chatting, e-streaming, e-navigating, e-shopping, e-planning, e-booking, e-paying, e-dating, e-socializing, e-gathering, e-consulting, e-matching, e-learning, e-gaming, e-gambling, e-crowd-funding, e-voting, e-protesting.

Along the same line, new challenges for businesses and other organizations emerged for improving their profits or functioning by optimizing their *cyber processes* like e-marketing, e-warehousing, e-banking, e-tracking, e-tracing, e-procuring, e-selling, e-renting, e-transporting, e-meeting, e-negotiating, e-participating, e-cooperating, e-supervising, e-teaching, e-governing, and e-crowd sourcing. Similarly, technology-driven companies and organizations in industry and (critical) infrastructures started their *operational technology (OT)-enabled activities* and *processes* like e-producing, e-supplying drinking water and energy, e-building, e-transporting, e-telesurgery performing, e-data acquisitioning, e-mining, e-monitoring, e-controlling, e-steering, e-supplying, and e-networking.

However, next to all these (growing) benefits, cyberspace suffers from existing and upcoming cyber threats due to our growing dependence on IT and OT. After all, both IT and OT, can unintentionally fail, or natural disasters can take place like hurricanes, floods, and earthquakes. Moreover, malicious people and organizations, from script kiddies, hackers, criminal gangs, to even state actors, can choose from a huge variety of e-means (including those available in the dark web [2]) to execute all kinds of annoying, odious, disruptive, criminal, et cetera e-activities, and e-processes like e-bullying, e-fraud committing, e-sexting, e-pornography distributing, e-fake news spreading, e-illegal goods selling, e-cyberattack services renting, e-espying, e-influencing, e-stealing, e-intelligence collecting, e-attacking, e-sabotaging, and even e-warfare operating.

As a consequence of the cyber threats related to cyber activities and processes, *cyber incidents* of all kind (can) occur with (potentially) high negative impact for individuals, businesses and organizations, up to governments, states, and in the darkest scenario's (e.g., due to a huge electricity blackout, or the shutdown of crucial Internet exchanges), even parts of continents. So, the *security of cyberspace*, that is, *cybersecurity* is at stake, and we have to deal with the existing and upcoming cyber risks in order to get the related *cybersecurity risk levels* at sufficient levels.

Based on these considerations, the *goals of this paper* are to more precisely define the present-day cybersecurity challenges, to analyze our current cyber resilience levels, and, finally, to sketch the cybersecurity solution directions needed to guarantee sufficient cybersecurity levels in all cyber subdomains.

1.2 Conceptualizing cyberspace and cybersecurity

To reach the goals defined above, we need to use a clear conceptualization of the domain at stake, that is, of cyberspace. In addition, we need to have a clear understanding of what cybersecurity entails. Both cyberspace (in which several billion people are active, facilitated by the worldwide Internet and other IT & OT) and cybersecurity are complex notions. Fortunately, we can use earlier research outcomes here. Due to various reasons, we were forced to come up with the first ideas around precisely defining cyberspace and cybersecurity almost fifteen years ago, which resulted in the first (best paper award-winning) publication on this subject [3]. Actually, the terminology used in subsection 1.1 above is completely in line with the concepts introduced in that paper.

Later on, we elaborated these first ideas, resulting in a series of additional papers published, the last, most extensive one being [4]. Meanwhile, the Dutch National Coordinator for Counterterrorism and Security (NCCS) of the Ministry of Justice and Security almost completely adopted our conceptualizations; see, for example, the "Cyber Security Assessment Netherlands (CSAN) 2013" report [5]. The elaboration of the first ideas resulted later in a set of additional *mental models* that more precisely define cyberspace and cybersecurity [4]. Here we confine ourselves to present the basic cyberspace model and basic cybersecurity model, and to briefly describe the set of additional mental models needed to understand the rest of this chapter.

The basic *three-layer Cyberspace Model* is shown in **Figure 1**. The middle layer is the *socio-technical layer*, that is, the layer of cyber activities and cyber processes. This middle layer concerns the most crucial layer (!), namely, that of the *key assets* of cyberspace, since it concerns the cyber activities and processes that people execute in order to achieve their specific goals, so it concerns *human behavior*. When acting in cyberspace by means of e-enabled cyber applications, users utilize IT & OT services of the "underlying" *technical layer* shown as the inner layer in **Figure 1**.

The choice of making a separation between the technical layer and the socio-technical layer has severe consequences—when we talk about *cybersecurity*, we mean the security of the cyber activities and cyber processes of the socio-technical layer, while if we speak about *information security*, we mean the security of the technical (inner) layer. The latter concerns the security of data that are being stored and processed in terms of the preservation of their confidentiality, integrity, and availability (CIA) (see, e.g., the famous ISO/IEC) 27,000-series on information security: [6] and its successor publications). Within this framework of thinking, it should be clear that information security incidents that take place in the technical layer pose threats to the cyber security of the socio-technical layer. This all implies that *information security management* is fundamentally different from *cyber security management*, both needing specific, complementary attention.

The third outer layer of the Cyberspace Model is the *governance layer,* the layer of rules and regulations that should be put in place to properly organize the two other

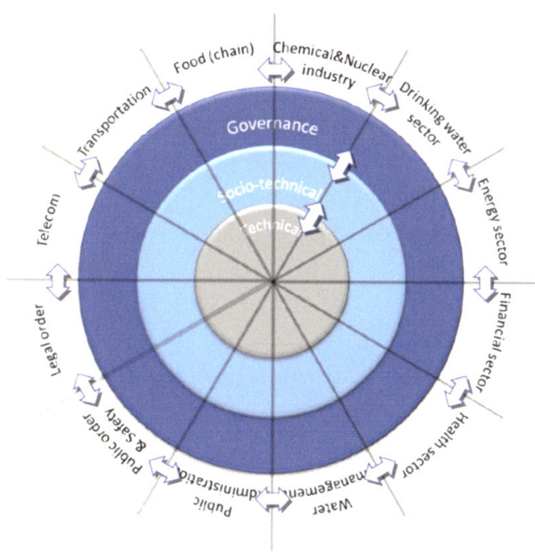

Figure 1.
Basic 3-layer cyberspace model [3, 4].

layers, including their security. This relates, for example, to the Internet governance issues related to the functioning of the World Wide Web and the Internet as a whole, next to rules and regulations that influence human cyber behavior, that is, the way people execute cyber activities and cyber processes in the middle layer.

Next to the separation into three layers, the cyberspace model of **Figure 1** shows a division in pie slices mentioning various *cyber subdomains*. This is done to emphasize that cyber activities and processes in different subdomains often have different characteristics and thus different cybersecurity challenges.

For each cyberspace layer, a specific *mental model* can be used to concisely describe its fundamental characteristics [4]. For the socio-technical layer, the basic challenge for people is to act "unconscious cyber competent" as "homo digitalis," that is, to show continuously and consistently adequate cyber(security) behavior. For the technical layer, the key issues relate to the two protocol stacks used to describe computer networks, namely the OSI and TCP/IP protocol stacks [7]. For the governance layer, the chosen mental model concerns the four modalities of regulation in cyberspace [8] (1) laws, rules, policies, & regulations, (2) norms, that is, informal societal rules, (3) markets, and (4) architecture, that is, physical or technical constraints on cyber activities. This framing of these four modalities of regulation of the governance layer is precisely in line with the three-layer model of cyberspace: the modalities of laws, norms, and markets steer cyber activities and processes, that is, steer cyber behavior from a direct governance perspective, while the modality architecture puts constraints on the cyber activities and processes by measures taken in the technical layer. For more digressions about these three specific mental models of cyberspace, we refer to [4].

Having visualized cyberspace, we now present the *basic bowtie model of cybersecurity*. Going from left to right in **Figure 2**, the model shows (intentional and unintentional) threats, incidents, and the impact of the latter. Threats may result in (sometimes interdependent) cyber incidents. Incidents occur with a certain probability or likelihood, and the risk of a cyber incident is defined as the expected impact of this incident, that is, *risk = likelihood x impact*. In cyberspace, the bowtie model can be used to model cyber threats, cyber incidents, and their (negative) impact, and thus cyber risks. To avoid cyber incidents happening, preventive measures can be taken to reduce the probability of their occurrence. To reduce the impact of occurring incidents, repressive measures should be taken. For more details on (the use of) the bowtie model, we refer to reference [9].

Cybersecurity is actually a risk management challenge. For proper risk management, a risk management process should be implemented (basically a responsibility

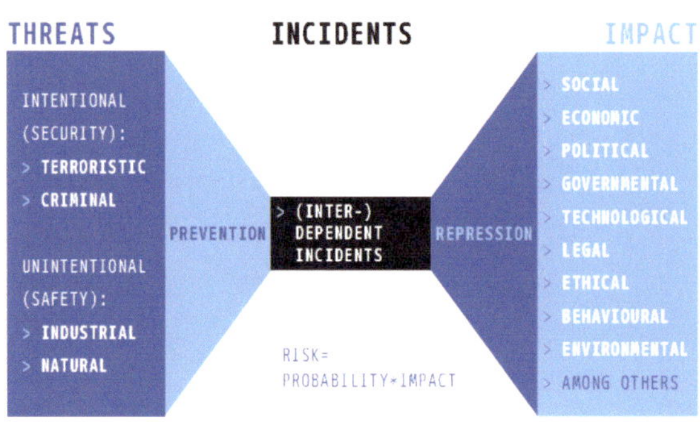

Figure 2.
Basic (bowtie) model of cybersecurity [3, 4]. (adapted from [9]).

of the governance actors). This process can be implemented as a *cyber risk management cycle* of six basic steps and can be described by the following pseudo-code: "Repeat forever, in all cyber subdomains, (1) identify critical cyber activities and processes (sometimes termed the "crown jewels"); (2) identify & assess their cyber risks (potential gains & losses); (3) define acceptable cyber risk levels; (4) decide way(s) of dealing with the risks; (5) design & implement relevant cyber risk measures; and (6) monitor the effectiveness of measures taken." Once again, we emphasize here that within our framework of thinking, cybersecurity primarily entails risk management of cyber activities and cyber processes. Since the characteristics of these activities and processes often vary substantially in different cyber subdomains and, therefore, the related cyber risks vary as well, cyber risk management cycle processes should be adapted to the actual context in which they are executed.

Like the cyberspace model, the bowtie cybersecurity model can be specified in more detail by means of a set of (additional) mental models [4]. These additional mental models will be briefly summarized here and relate to the six steps of the risk management cycle: (1) the "crown jewels model" (to describe the critical cyber activities and processes at stake), (2) the "cyber situation awareness" model (to know and understand goal and progress of actual cyber activities and processes) and the "unified kill chain model" (to identify the related intentional and unintentional cyber threats and the ways in which cyberattacks take place), (3) the "risk matrix model" (to assess the related cyber risks), (4) the "risk response strategies model" (to select the proper way(s) of dealing with the established cyber risks), (5) the "Swiss cheese model," the "institutional design" model and the "cyber social contract model" (to select the concrete measures of dealing with the cyber risks), (6) the "cyber situational awareness model" again (to understand the behavior changes of running cyber activities and processes as a result of the measures taken). For more contemplations about these additional mental models for implementing the cyber risk management cycle, we refer again to [4].

1.3 Methodological remarks

The first group of remarks concerns the domain focus of the research executed or, more precisely, concerns the cyberspace areas in the world we selected to focus on. Since the ways cyberspace is managed and governed often very differ in various countries (mainly due to existing distinct political opinions and structures), we observe that (a) cyber activities and processes in the world differ, and (b) what is considered cybersecurity and the way it is implemented certainly differs. In this book chapter, we mainly focus on countries having a so-called "open society" [10]. This choice is also motivated by the fact that sources with recent information about current cyber(security) developments and practices are easier to find in these countries.

A second group of remarks concerns the chosen research approach. As already mentioned in the introduction, we used the earlier developed concepts of cyberspace and cybersecurity as a "*lens*" to sketch and analyze current cyber and cybersecurity developments. By using this lens, we actually apply a *transdisciplinary* [11] research strategy crossing various disciplinary boundaries (e.g., we talk about human behavior, technologies, and legislation) and based on both scientific and practical sources. Especially the latter enabled us to use information sources describing very recent developments. Other characteristics of our research approach are a socio-technical view (i.e., considering the interrelation of social and technical aspects) and a multi-actor view (we include all actors in cyberspace, in possibly various roles), which altogether results in a holistic picture [11] ("the whole is greater than the sum of the parts").

A third group of remarks concerns *validation*—is the applied methodology a correct one? We do think so, because our conceptualizations of cyberspace and cybersecurity have already been successfully applied in designing and implementing an executive master's program cybersecurity, in many master's thesis research projects (for examples, see ref. [4]), and in cybersecurity research resulting in scientific papers published (see [3, 4], and the references in [4]). Also, the adoption in 2021 of our conceptual framework by the Dutch Ministry of Justice and Security for creating the yearly CSAN reports underpins the effectiveness of our way of thinking.

Our final methodological remarks are also validation-related. Using the terms of our conceptualizations of cyberspace and its security, we searched on the Internet for information sources. To double-check the validity of factual findings, we often searched for additional sources. The resulting conclusions in Sections 5 and 6 followed mostly from logical inferences in the text and have, as much as possible, been checked using information from additional trustworthy sources.

1.4 Structure of the remainder of this chapter

In order to create a more complete overview of present-day cyberspace dynamics, Section 2 presents additional examples of currently widely used, new, and emerging cyber activities and processes. Section 3 then first provides a series of mostly recent cyber incidents (and related cyber threats and impact), from which we next derive present-day cybersecurity challenges. We continue by sketching actual cyber resilience levels in Section 4. By combining all this information, we present in Section 5 a set of solution directions needed to create desired cyber risk levels in the various cyber subdomains. Finally, Section 6 summarizes our findings by means of a few main conclusions.

2. Present-day cyber activities and processes

In the introductory section, we already sketched examples of various (IT- & OT-based) cyber activities and processes. Based on various (other) sources, we here elaborate on this to create a more complete, up-to-date picture of cyberspace developments by sketching currently widely used, new, and emerging e-activities and processes as executed by various stakeholders.

a. Considering *individual end-users* in cyberspace, we first provide a set of *key statistics* (i.e., estimations of their Internet-based activities) [12]: "There are (currently) 5.35 billion Internet users worldwide," "On average, Internet users spend six and a half hours online every day," "75% of people aged 15–24 have access to the Internet across the world," "7.5 million blog posts are published each day," and "5.04 billion people are on social media as of 2024." Especially (free of charge) social media like Facebook, TikTok, Twitter, and Instagram are extremely popular, since they enable user-friendly "multimodal communication, simultaneously with many members" [13]. They are mostly used for private information exchange, but sometimes also for more professional reasons, as in the case of LinkedIn and YouTube. Another important motivation is financial: content creators or influencers (i.e., persons with a large group of followers) are contacted by large companies to promote their products or apply affiliate marketing. It is further important to note that in many cases these social media are used anonymously, for example, by adopting a nickname or various fake names.

Talking about Internet use, we should also briefly discuss the existence of the *surface web* ("representing about 5% of its total content"), the *deep web* ("representing about 90% of its total content" and concerns the websites "used by entities such as corporations, government agencies, and nonprofits"), and the *dark web* ("representing about 5% of its total content" and concerns "an area of the Internet that is only accessible by users who have a Tor browser installed") [14]. The original goal of using the Tor browser was to enable Internet users to privately browse without tracking, surveillance, or censorship. It is currently mostly known as a cyber area where illegal goods and services can be obtained.

Another Internet source [15] mentions the currently *"ten most-used" general cyber activities* of end-users being social networking, online shopping, online banking, e-education and upskilling, e-gaming, e-trading, e-dating, e-mailing, e-newspaper reading, and e-researching. Going into more detail of cyber activities, we observe the still great popularity of e-trade in cryptocurrencies like Bitcoin, Ethereum, Tether USDt, BNB, and Solana, among almost 200 others [16]. Maybe somewhat less-known, we observe Internet of Things-(IoT-) based cyber activities and processes like e-monitoring of personal health, water and energy use at home, e-tracking of solar energy production [17], and e-controlling distant home temperatures and security. Note that for quite some cyber activities, end-users do not communicate with human beings but just with "intelligent servers," for example, when performing e-transactions or talking with chatbots. The latter Artificial Intelligence (AI)-based service relates to the recent revolutionary growth of generative AI-based ("human creativity empowering") products and tools [18] enabling the e-creation or adaption of images, music, video's, text, and computer code, with probably the most well-known example tool ChatGPT [19]. The latter can be used for answering questions, generating content, translating languages, writing computer code, engaging in conversations, and providing explanations, among others.

b. Considering *businesses and other organizations* acting in cyberspace, we observe (and experience) that the digitization of business processes also continues and deepens, often driven by financial motives. When searching for present-day *e-commerce trends*, we found 12 trends that are "powering online retail forward" like augmented reality in online shopping, voice search facilities, chatbot-enabled personalized product recommending, chat-marketing, mobile shopping services, flexible payment solutions, e-shopping via social media platforms, personalized price offerings, and more [20]. But also in other sectors like finance, agriculture and livestock farming, public and commercial transporting, water supply, and other critical infrastructures (just to name a few), we see all kinds of new Internet-enabled solutions related to enhancing efficiency, convenience, quality control, sustainability, or security.

In industrial contexts, digitalization is further developing using technologies like IoT and cloud computing. Examples of IoT-based applications in subdomains like agriculture, logistics, retail, and transportation include e-monitoring and e-management of micro-climate conditions in greenhouses, e-tracking of products from their start on the factory floor to their placement in the destination store, e-controlling warehouse automation and robotics by (online and in-store) shopping sales figures, e-steering of self-driving cars, and (sensor data-based) e-improving of fleet vehicle driving behavior resulting into optimized performance, fuel use reduction, and reduced pollution generation [17]. Note that also here more and more AI-based solutions have been adopted.

Examples of present-day cloud-based applications in industry and beyond include big data storage, management & analysis, corporate solutions for e-commerce, marketing & sales, scalable and adaptable cloud services for software testing, e-services for presentation and video-conferencing, and real-time daily accounting services [21].

c. Considering the digital transformation in *governments and state actors*, it refers to processes of utilizing technology and digital solutions to modernize and enhance the delivery of public services and to streamline internal operations (both in the socio-technical layer of the cyberspace model) and to improve overall governance [22]. This of course also concerns intense transformation processes. It aims to facilitate data-driven decision making, to realize citizen-centric servicing, to promote transparency and accountability in day-to-day operations, and to safe costs and enhance operational efficiency, among others [20]. More specifically, we observe e-based measures to streamline public and private mobility, to accelerate the energy transition, and to improve biodiversity, sustainability, and other environmental-related affairs, often within the context of creating smart cities and environments.

Considering the governmental task of creating and maintaining a safe and secure "open society" [10], lots of e-enabled initiatives are being taken, from managing the safety of large crowds and high traffic volumes, protecting critical infrastructure, law enforcement on the street, reducing trade in hard drugs, unmasking financial fraud, and enhancing national intelligence efforts for detecting intellectual property stealing, fake news spreading, and terrorism and warfare-related attacks. In non-open societies, those in power interpret their safety and security role usually very differently and use their IT-enabled capabilities (also) to impose a single ideology, suppress individual freedoms, detect and prohibit critical organizations, and track, trace, arrest, and convict dissidents, among others.

As a final remark related to present-day cyber activities and operations, it is important to note that the underlying, enabling transnational IT & OT services of the technical layer are often under the control of a small group of providers, ranging from basic Internet communication services (like satellite-based Starlink [23]) to cloud-based services and applications in the possession of big companies (like the five Tech Titans and big Chinese IT companies [24]).

3. Actual cybersecurity challenges

Having sketched above an updated picture of the current cyber activities and processes, we here continue by presenting the related cybersecurity challenges. We first present an overview of recent cyber incidents in various cyber subdomains, including the related (un)intentional threats and impacts (remember the bowtie model). Secondly, we derive from this a list of actual cybersecurity challenges.

3.1 Recent cyber incidents

When searching on the Internet for recent cyber incidents, you can easily find large numbers of websites, papers, and reports presenting a wide variety of incidents. To structure our search efforts, we first looked for information about single incidents with (potentially) big impact. Next, we searched for sources providing more structured information in terms of overviews and trends.

Let us start with a very recent, truly "wake-up call" incident: July 19, 2024, a defect CrowdStrike content update hit over 8.5 million Windows hosts impacting a range of industries with flights grounded, health services affected, and payment services unavailable; see Reference [25] for details, and its Internet links. This cyber incident is considered one of the worst cases ever due to its enormous impact. Maybe surprising—it was an unintentional attack. The same source also mentions details of another big incident named "RockYou2024," where a hacker exposed nearly 10 billion passwords. The potential harm (impact) of this incident is huge since threat actors could use the information in the RockYou file "to conduct brute-force attacks and gain unauthorized access to various online accounts used by individuals who employ passwords" [25]. To refresh our memory (occurred cyber incidents are often quickly forgotten), we also looked for the biggest cyber incidents ever and their impact. We found a list of ten incidents [26] and describe here six of them: (1) 1999 Melissa virus incident (causing widespread disruption of operations at major companies and the US Army), (2) 2023 MOVEit incident (the related zero-day vulnerability-based attack in question affected over 2000 organizations and exposed the data of 60 million people), (3) 1999 NASA cyber incident (a 15-year-old computer hacker caused a 21-day shutdown of NASA computers that support the International Space Station and invaded a Pentagon weapons computer system), (4) 2007 Estonia Cyber Attack (a Russian state-based Distributed Denial-of-Service (DDoS) attack against critical infrastructures of Estonia disrupted essential services like online banking, media communication, and government functions), and (5) 2011 PlayStation Network incident (hackers infiltrated Sony's PlayStation Network resulting in the theft of personal information from about 77 million user accounts), and (6) 2015 Ukraine Power Grid incident (the related malware based attack is considered the first successful cyberattack to cause a power outage on a national grid, resulting in power outages for around 230,000 customers). During the ongoing Russo-Ukrainian War (started in 2022), there have been multiple cyberattacks targeting Ukraine's national infrastructure. For more details about these and other big incidents, we refer to Reference [26].

Since social networking is the greatest cyber activity (see above), we also searched for cyber incidents that occur in this cyber subdomain. It is easy to find information sources discussing cyber activities like cyberbullying, cyberstalking, cyber harassment, and victimization leading to incidents related to poor workplace performance, psychological distress, and social isolation, among others (see ref. [27] for example). Social media are often also used in other undesirable ways, for example to spread misinformation, fake news, and unwanted pornographic videos, to create social media addiction, to distract and create productivity losses, and to compromise user privacy and expose users to fraud [28]. Moreover, we found that Internet-enabled social networks not only directly suffer from cyber incidents; the related social media are also exploited as a "social engineering" channel, that is, as a means, to cause cyber incidents in other cyber subdomains by means of (enhanced spear-) phishing attacks [29].

We already mentioned the existence of the notorious dark web that enables, by allowing anonymous acting, all kinds of illegal activities. It is quite easy to find (on the normal surf web) horror stories with details on dark cyber incidents with big impact related to criminal activities like buying and selling illegal drugs, weapons, passwords and stolen identities, and trading illegal (child) pornography.

Having presented this overview of cyber incidents, we observe that (a) the numbers are high, (b) most incidents occur due to intentional attacks, (c) attacker types (still) range from script kiddies to cybercriminals and state actors, (d) impacts range from personal harm to disruptions of critical infrastructures, which can affect thousands of people, and, therefore, (e) the impact of a single incident is sometimes enormous.

In order to check and validate the findings presented in this subsection, we also inspected information sources discussing general cyber security developments and trends. First, we reread the developments and trends as reported in the recent CSAN reports earlier mentioned ([5] and other versions). They confirm our observation that cybercriminals and state actors (notably Russia and China) create the biggest threat for open societies. The primary motive for cybercriminals is financial gain, and for state actors, geopolitical and economic gain. Both types of actors permanently invent new ways and apply new (sometimes in the dark web hired) tools to execute their attacks. Especially ransomware-based attacks are a big threat for national security in terms of the continuity of vital processes and for keeping sensitive and private information secure. The reason that cybercriminals can be so sophisticated in their cyberattacks is that they are usually well organized, often by acting in the dark web, where they can make use of cyber-as-a-crime services and communicate unnoticed. Next to ransomware, Distributed Denial-of-Service (DDOS) software is used as an attacking tool within the context of current geopolitical tensions and warfare operations. These and other general findings are illustrated in the CSAN reports by means of lists of occurred cyber incidents. In a categorization of these, we observed, as remarkable types of cyber incidents, cyber espionage incidents, cyber sabotage incidents, website defacement incidents, supply chain information disruption incidents, and process disruption incidents. The incidents and types reported are largely in line with the cyber incidents mentioned earlier and in the first paragraphs of this subsection.

In a final attempt to get improved insights about recent cyberspace incidents, we used the Google browser with the key words "general cyber developments and trends." The first results presented information about cyber war trends and technologies with discussions on cyber warfare operations (intelligence, defense, and attack) and hybrid warfare (merging traditional military action with cyberattack operations) [30]. Another paper [31] presents the results of analysis of around 15 million cyberattacks mentioning trends like "cyber espionage is most likely aiming government, media, and law enforcement sectors," "cyber espionage, cyber war and hacktivism techniques, cyber-crime target all business sectors," and "there is a continuous increase in the mobile attacks" (i.e., attacks resulting into unauthorized access to smart phones).

As a side-remark at the end of this subsection, we observe that the inspected information sources use the concepts of cyberspace and cybersecurity usually with a meaning different from ours and from each other, or not define them at all. For example, cyberspace is seldom defined, the terms cyber activities and cyber processes are rarely found, while cybersecurity and information security are often treated as synonyms (then having the classical meaning of the "security of data," as promoted by the famous ISO/IEC-27000-series [6]). More in general are cyber concepts often used in sloppy ways: cyber risks are regularly correctly considered as risks, but often (also) as probabilities of an incident, and malware like ransomware is often termed an attack, or even an incident, instead of a means to execute an attack that may result in a cyber incident.

3.2 Cybersecurity challenges

Having presented an updated image of occurring cyber incidents, we can derive from these the related cybersecurity challenges, both general and specific ones. To structure the information presented below, general challenges will be numbered by adding a single number x, written in the text as (x), with x = 1, 2, ..., while more specific challenges will be numbered with more numbers and written like (2.1), (2.2), ... and (3.1.1), (3.1.2)....

Remembering the introduced cyberspace model, we defined cybersecurity as the security of all cyber activities and processes (as initiated and executed by the various cyberspace actors in their different cyber roles), and the main goal of cybersecurity is to bring the security in all cyberspace subdomains at acceptable levels. This overall cybersecurity challenge can be better understood by considering each step of the cyber risk management cycle discussed in Section 1. Since cyberspace actors are very often unexpectedly surprised by occurring cyber incidents, we observe that a lot of them apparently not correctly (and sometimes not at all) implemented the cyber risk management cycle. This may relate to the relative novelty and high dynamics of cyberspace and related risks, as well as the lack of knowledge how to do or organize this. The latter is understandable since most steps of the cyber risk management cycle, actually from 2 till 6, are hard to do for an individual cyberspace actor, and support for doing so is often hard to find. Looking more specifically to step 3 (of defining acceptable cyber risk levels for all cyber activities and processes), we note that the latter is actually not a question that science can easily answer, but more a question that should be dealt with by all stakeholders themselves; for example, end-users should themselves define the acceptable cybersecurity risk levels for the cyber activities they execute in their private, work, school, and leisure time environment. For lots of businesses and other organizations, including governmental ones, especially the big ones, we experienced that a lot of them have already difficulties with step 1 of the cycle to define their digital crown jewels and therefore as well to precisely define in step 3 the acceptable cyber risk levels for these crown jewels. In addition, it is often hard to assess (in step 2) present-day cyber risks because, in order to do so, a lot of experience is needed. Related to this have many cyber actors difficulties in taking on (in step 5) the preventive and repressive measures needed, and just do whatever comes to mind. The fact that both people and organizations are often surprised by the sudden occurrence of high-impact incidents further suggests that lots of them paid too little attention to repressive measures (right-hand side of the bowtie), since such measures could have reduced the impact of such incidents. From these observations, it is clear that a first general cyber security challenge (1) is to provide cyberspace actors, in their various roles, with sufficient knowledge and skills to apply adequate cyber risk management.

Looking at the group of end-users, the general cybersecurity challenge (2) is the accomplishment of secure cyber behavior with respect to their cyber activities in various cyber subdomains. As a first example, we take a look at e-enabled social networking. The various incident types described in subsection 3.1 make clear that the e-enabled social networking environments are far from secure. The related challenge (2.1) is therefore to transform those environments into ones where people feel themselves safe and secure in all possible ways, which implies that they themselves behave according to agreed conventions, rules, and regulations. Similar challenges (2.2), (2.3), ... can of course be formulated for a lot of other e-enabled environments related to school, work, traveling, and leisure.

Looking at businesses and other organizations, the main cybersecurity challenge (3) is to keep their e-business processes sufficiently secure and thus sufficiently resistant against intentional and unintentional, internal and external threats. These threats concern both malicious individuals and organizations (from their own employees to monetary motive-driven hackers and competitors) who execute cyber-attacks. But they also concern (information security) threats from the underlying IT & OT services that may themselves (un)intentionally be disrupted or fail. Actually, we talk here about large numbers of cyber subdomains with very specific characteristics, which results in specific cybersecurity challenges (3.1), (3.2), ... for each cyber subdomain. It should be clear that the top managers of these organizations are the true responsible persons to formulate and deal with these domain-specific cybersecurity challenges.

We do not further elaborate here the cybersecurity challenges per cyber subdomain, simply because they are too numerous. Instead, we inspected again the (high-impact) cyber incidents described above and brought to mind here that, within the current geopolitical climate, cyber threats also come from abroad, both intentional, like in the context of international business competition or military conflicts, and unintentional, in the context of failures of global IT or OT services. So, we add, as a relatively general additional cybersecurity challenge for businesses and other organizations, the challenge (4) to adequately deal with the cyber threats from abroad with an aim to stay sufficiently cybersecure.

Thinking about cybersecurity challenges for government, we first observe that both for their internal operations and for critical infrastructures the same observations hold as those described in the previous two paragraphs, so this again concerns challenges (3.1), (3.2), ..., and (4). But, in addition, we know that governments have the general governance task of making and keeping the relevant parts of cyberspace sufficiently secure (challenge (5)), based on their social contracts with citizens, companies, and other organizations [4]. This concerns again, like for businesses and other organizations, two complementary challenges, the first one (5.1) being the information security of all IT and OT infrastructures in use (layer 1 of the cyberspace model), the second one (5.2) the security of cyber activities and processes in cyber subdomains (layer 2).

Elaborating the two complementary challenges, we observe that the information security challenge (5.1) concerns the cybersecurity governance of both (the underlying) Internet (5.1.1) and the (higher level) IT- and OT-platform services, as made available by (mainly the big) IT companies (5.1.2). At the lowest level of the information security challenge (5.1.1), we should pay attention to the availability of sufficient, secure hardware. Also here, geopolitical tensions play a role related to the scarcity of certain essential raw materials, the production of microchips (see ref. [32] for example, the ASML case), and the potential insecurity of essential hardwired devices (like the controversy around 5G network devices coming from China [33]). With respect to the higher layers in the Internet protocol stack, we see that global Internet governance is conducted "by a decentralized and international multistakeholder network of interconnected autonomous groups." These groups aim "to create shared policies and standards that maintain the Internet's global interoperability for the public good" [34]. Originally, they (successfully) focused on technical issues like the establishment of unique domain names, IP addresses, and protocols. However, later on, other principles such as freedom of expression, freedom of information and human rights have been adopted by the multistakeholder network. These principles actually concern the cybersecurity challenges (2.1), (2.2), ..., where the bad news is that there exist huge international disagreements over what these principles practically mean and imply.

The information security challenge (5.1.2) of securing the (higher level) IT- and OT-platform services relates to cloud- and IoT-technologies. Concrete issues involve reducing dependency on services of the major IT companies, creating fair and transparent free market conditions for these (without monopolies), and enforcing compliance with the law (for example, related to privacy preservation and counteracting vendor lock-in).

The governmental challenge (5.2) of securing cyber activities and processes in all cyber subdomains is even a bigger one. It implies that citizens of all ages should become competent cybersecure actors, homo digitalis, and that governments have the task to design and implement a national cybersecurity strategy and related action plan (5.2.1) with concrete elaborations in terms of additional cyber education, stimulation, support, and enforcement. Similarly, and also part of the strategy and action plan, business and organizations (including the ones belonging to the government itself) should be supported and enforced to act and process cybersecurity (5.2.2). The four modalities of IT regulation [8] mentioned in Section 1 of this chapter certainly apply here.

The safeguarding of cyberspace also requires the creation of better cyber situational awareness (knowing and understanding what 24/7 is happening in relevant cyberspace subdomains [4]), based on which governments more continuously can assess actual cyber risks and inform the public about this. A final important governmental task concerns the institutional design of a cybersecurity governance ecosystem (with arrangements between actors that regulate cybersecurity tasks, responsibilities, costs, benefits, and risks [4]), with adequate governmental supervision.

4. Actual cyber resilience levels

When cyberspace for everyone suddenly emerged at the end of the previous century, cyber skills were generally low and cyber resilience a nonexistent term. But shaken awake by a growing number of incidents, cybersecurity awareness started to increase gradually and, supported by campaigns, trainings and discussions, cybersecurity behavior to improve little by little. Actually, a kind of cybersecurity rat race emerged where attackers enhanced and refined their attacks (see ref. [4] for eaxmple, the "unified kill chain model"), and, as a reaction, cyber actors improved their defensive cybersecurity practices (which, in their turn, stimulated attackers to further sophisticate their attack strategies, and so on and so on). As a consequence of these dynamics between cyber attackers and defenders, we note that cyber resilience levels are not fixed but change over time. So, it is hard to know precisely how high these levels are today. Therefore, we decided not to assess their precise levels but, instead, to just describe observed trends in the efforts defenders make to secure their digital activities and processes.

The rat race mentioned above is certainly visible for the group of end-users. Supported by the availability of various defense tools (like advanced virus detection tools) and the enforcement of two-factor authentication and other security practices by e-services providers, end-users now more regularly install software updates, backup their data, and show improved cyber behavior. Being better aware of the risks, end-users also act more cautious, for example, when reading emails (with possibly phishing intentions), participating in social networks, performing transactions during e-shopping or e-booking activities, or being called by a supposedly bank employee who asks for login details. When surfing via open communication channels, growing numbers of people (especially those living in countries without freedom of speech and press) make use of a Virtual Private Network (VPN) connection (to hide their cyber activities from others). In addition, they pay more security attention when installing IoT devices or uploading handy smart phone apps.

On a larger scale, the same trends are visible for businesses and other organizations, including governmental institutions, where the bigger ones usually do better. The related cyber security endeavors are not only motivated by their own cyber risk assessments but also through enforcement by national and internal rules and regulations. In Europe, for example, the 2016 General Data Protection Regulation (GDPR) set strong guidelines for the collection and processing of personal information from individuals. These guidelines are compulsory for businesses and other organizations acting in one of the European Union (EU) countries and have a huge impact. Probably even more influential is the 2023 Network and Information Security Directive 2 (NIS2). It obligates medium-sized and large companies, as well as organizations working in one of seven essential sectors, to "strengthen the security requirements, address the security of supply chains, streamline (cyber incident) reporting obligations," among others. More specifically for companies that produce devices with digital elements, the 2022 Cyber Resilience Act (CSR) is of importance. It prescribes that digital devices should be designed in such a way that those receiving automatic updates should also receive automatic security updates. Those companies should furthermore conduct cyber risk assessments for their products and report occurring cyber incidents. For more details about these and many other cybersecurity regulations, mostly of western countries, we refer to [35] and its numerous references.

With respect to governmental institutions, similar trends as described in the previous paragraph hold for their e-enabled processes. With respect to NIS2, national governments do have additional obligations like adopting a national cybersecurity strategy and action plan (for an example see ref. [36]), participating in coordinated vulnerability disclosures by fixing them in a European registry, ensuring that measures of supervision or enforcement are effective, proportionate, and dissuasive, and ensuring the imposition of administrative fines, among others. This also involves the monitoring of the big IT companies and the requirement to act in cases they transgress the applicable cyber rules or regulations. Concrete cases, for example, related to the GDPR legislation [37], show that governments do enforce cyber legislation, but the fines issued are mostly incomparable and small compared to the (huge) profits of those companies.

With respect to the governmental task of creating cyber situational awareness that helps to enhance cyber resilience, complications exist since governments should themselves behave compliant with existing cyber legislation [35], for example with respect to the privacy of people. This creates limitations to what extent governments can track and trace people. Another complication here is that illegal and criminal activities are often executed on the dark web. Of course, national intelligence services and other security companies are very active here, but they are generally not very transparent in what they know and discover, which, in turn, thwarts citizens and business organizations from understanding actual cyber risks.

A very recent development concerns the governmental effort to deal with generative AI-related security problems. Next to the many benefits (see also Section 2) generative AI may "affect public values such as non-discrimination, privacy, and transparency. If it leads to the deterioration of our information ecosystem, it thereby affects democracy and our rule of law" [38]. We are also aware of many discussions on the relationship between intellectual property rights and generative AI. Reference [38] of the Dutch Ministry of Internal Affairs further provides a list of six action lines to deal with generative AI, like "closely monitoring all developments," "shaping and applying laws and regulations," and "strong and clear supervision and enforcement," which actually shows that governments still struggle with the control over this new cyber development.

More generally, we may conclude from this and other examples that, due to the fast emergence of new cyber activities and processes and the much lower speed of new cyber law adoption, cyber security legislation is at various stages of implementation and often not yet adapted to the newest cyber security challenges.

5. Cybersecurity solution directions

Having created updated pictures of actual cybersecurity challenges and cyber resilience levels, we can now sketch cybersecurity solution directions. Remembering the list of recent cybersecurity incidents, we start by bringing to mind that solutions that guarantee 100% security are not available and that we always should prepare for unexpected cybersecurity breaches. This is often compactly framed as "expect the unexpected." So, solutions always have their limitations.

To formulate our set of solution directions, we return to the cybersecurity challenges of Section 3 and analyze to what extent they are dealt with by the actual cyber resilience efforts presented in Section 4. In the background, we also keep in mind the various cyber incidents mentioned in subsection 3.1.

The first general cyber security challenge (1) was formulated as "to provide cyberspace actors, in their various roles, with sufficient knowledge and skills to apply *adequate cyber risk management.*" Analyzing the actual cyber resilience efforts, we observe that, although much progress has been made in awareness and skills, cybersecurity risk capabilities and practices of people need to be further improved. This might be achieved to stimulate them, both at home, work or whatever environment, to better think through the kinds of cyber risks they may face when executing their cyber activities. This should result in *internalized cybersecurity behavior,* like installing antivirus software, always locking your computer when leaving your workplace, prompt installation of critical software updates, and making regular backups with a frequency adapted to the identified cyber risks. And for those installing IoT devices, they should automatically pay attention to the related cybersecurity risks.

Also, businesses and other organizations are doing better nowadays, but many of them do not have a sufficiently developed corporate culture around cybersecurity management, with clear responsibilities for the various employees under the umbrella of a companywide cybersecurity strategy. In addition, we observe that governments are now taking up the cybersecurity risk management challenge (more) seriously, but the implementation of a cybersecurity governance ecosystem serving the whole country with clear cybersecurity responsibilities and supportive laws and regulations is far from complete. Regarding the design and implementation of a trustworthy cyber social contract between governments and civilians (which anchors what cybersecurity responsibilities governments take upon for companies and civilians in exchange for certain obligations of the latter), we only observe first attempts. We conclude that cybersecurity challenge (1) still holds and requires action in all cyber subdomains by all cyber actors in the three layers of cyberspace.

The general cybersecurity challenge (2) was formulated for end-users and expressed as "the accomplishment of *secure cyber behavior* with respect to their cyber activities in various cyber subdomains." Although also here improvements are visible (see Section 4), we see that cyber behavior in various contexts, like social networking, is far from inherently secure. To compare, if persons nowadays participate in traffic as pedestrian, biker, car driver, or whatsoever, most of them are very aware of the risks in all kinds of circumstances and show secure traffic behavior adapted to the actual situation; they internalized secure behavior in traffic. This level of security behavior should also be achieved in cyberspace and should be stimulated, and often even enforced in the various cyber subdomains. As an enforcement example let us assume, in a (unfortunately unrealistic) thought experiment, that we could get global agreement on a ban on anonymous cyber participation in social networks or other worldwide cyber environment, then their adoption would certainly substantially reduce the number of cyber incidents for individuals, companies and even states. The assumption of getting global agreement is unfortunately not feasible for such global cyber environments, but in other, smaller cyber subdomains, agreement might be reached and could a ban on anonymous cyber behavior be an effective enforcing measure.

The cybersecurity challenge (3) for business and other organizations was expressed as "to keep their *e-business processes sufficiently secure*, and thus sufficiently resistant against intentional and unintentional, internal and external threats." This challenge *also holds for governments* with respect to their internal operations. And again, we observe that progress is being made here, certainly regarding security awareness, but issues like the realization of internalized cybersecure behavior and cybersecure business processes, and law compliance are still often not sufficiently dealt with. Actually, we observe here also doubtful developments like the outsourcing of IT services to (what are sometimes termed) "hyperscalers" that offer large-scale data processing and data storage services [38].

The state-of-the art concerning general cybersecurity challenge (4) "to adequately deal with the *cyber threats from abroad* with aim to stay sufficiently cybersecure," which was formulated for both business and governments, may considered as probably one of the most disturbing. The underlying reason is that most of the cyberattacks are being executed by state actors and internationally organized criminals, and the amount and intensity of these attacks is expected to only increase in the coming years. The very up-to-date information on significant cyber incidents actually substantiates this claim; see reference [39, 40] and similar sources.

Cyber security challenge (5) for governments was decomposed in an information security challenge (5.1) concerning the *governance of national and international IT & OT infrastructures*, and the governmental challenge (5.2) of *securing cyber activities and processes in all cyber subdomains*. These concern both huge challenges, which can only successfully be dealt with in an international context. It would be of great value if the United Nations organization could get a leading role here, for example, as mediator in international cyberwar-related conflicts and in efforts to reduce international crimes (for example, with respect to what happens in the dark web), but we should notice here that this solution direction is currently also difficult to achieve due to geopolitical tensions.

A prerequisite for challenge (5.1) is to intensify the efforts in international forums to get agreement on how the dependence and power of the big IT companies (for example, in the ways they retain customers, stimulate screen addiction, and deal with their personal data) should be kept within acceptable limits. The good news is that the EU is taking these challenges seriously and often starts new initiatives, for example, by adopting and enforcing new cybersecurity legislation and by taking action against big companies who break the rules. The bad news, however, is that the current geopolitical tensions also here thwart global agreements regarding these challenges and actually invite for all kinds of new cyber conflicts. Governmental challenge (5.2) involves as the very first step the adoption and true implementation of a national cyber security strategy and related action plan, next to many more initiatives as described above.

6. Conclusions

In this final section, we confine ourselves to providing *a few main conclusions* concerning the goals of this chapter and some additional findings.

The choice of using the three-layer Cyberspace Model and the Cybersecurity Bowtie Model to frame our thoughts and observations appeared again to be very effective. Especially the *separation between the concept of information security* and *that of cyber security is crucial* to formulate challenges and solution directions in *behavioral and technical terms* that *everybody can understand*. This is actually in stark contrast to the conceptualizations used in the popular ISO/IEC 27000-series on information security [6], where the security of data and information (in the abstract terms of confidentiality, integrity, and availability) is the starting point. The latter results into information security management solutions that are almost solely understandable for specialized IT-security management persons. Our first conclusion is therefore:

- The ISO/IEC 27000-series [6] need to be rewritten, where cyber activities and cyber processes are defined as the key assets to be sufficiently secured.

The choice of adopting a multi-actor approach in the Cyberspace Model helped to formulate *actual cybersecurity challenges* for *three groups of cyber actors* being end-users, businesses and other organizations, and governments. These challenges can be framed in terms of behavioral influence toward internalized secure cyber behavior, and toward adequate cyber risk management (at home, work, school, ...), the creation of a corporate cyber security culture (in companies and other organizations including governmental institutions), and the development and implementation of a national cyber security strategy with accompanying action plan, where much attention is paid to international cyber threats. In this chapter, we have only been able to sketch the actual cybersecurity challenges in relatively general terms. We, therefore, formulate our second main conclusion as:

- The actual cybersecurity challenges described should be further concretized by the different cyber actor groups.

In the section on *cyber resilience*, we observed that in general all cyberspace actors are showing improvements; individuals do show more awareness and improved cybersecurity behavior, so do business and other organizations. Also, governments are taken cyberspace as new fifth domain seriously nowadays, and started to implement cybersecurity related regulations that are highly needed. But because of the sometimes still very unexpected occurrence of new cyber incidents, it is clear that the enhancement of cyber resilience levels still needs our attention, where taking repressive measures to limit the impact of occurring incidents should not be forgotten. We therefore also conclude that.

- Cyber resilience capabilities of all actors in cyberspace need to be further refined toward fully internalized cyber resilience behavior.

In the previous section on solution directions, we observed that these involve the continuation of the efforts of taking on the cybersecurity challenges of all cyber actors. Compared to say 10–20 years ago, we observe a society that is (a) much more active in cyberspace because of its benefits, but also (b) much more aware of (potentially) negative aspects. What we possibly mostly need to do now is to organize more discussions on what is happening cyberspace, what we think is correct and incorrect behavior, what cyber threats exist and related risks are, and what cybersecurity measures everyone can and should take to deal with these risks. This leads to the final conclusion formulated as:

- Let us all take cyberspace as separate fifth domain very seriously and organize more discussions, both nationally as internationally, on how we wish and should (securely) behave ourselves in this exciting domain.

Acknowledgements

I would like to express here my sincere thanks to IntechOpen for their kind invitation to compose this chapter and for their active funding support.

Author details

Jan van den Berg[1,2]

1 Faculty of Electrical Engineering, Mathematics and Computer Science and Faculty of Technology, Policy and Management, Delft University of Technology, Delft, The Netherlands

2 Faculty of Governance and Global Affairs, Leiden University, The Hague, The Netherlands

*Address all correspondence to: j.vandenberg@tudelft.nl

References

[1] Pagamini P. NATO officially recognizes cyberspace a warfare domain [Internet]. 2017. Available from: https://securityaffairs.com/48484/cyber-warfare-2/nato-cyberspace-warfare-domain.html [Accessed: July 19, 2024]

[2] Dark web [Internet]. Wikipedia. 2024. Available from: https://en.wikipedia.org/wiki/Dark_web [Accessed: July 27, 2024]

[3] Van den Berg J, Van Zoggel J, Snels M, Van Leeuwen M, Boeke S, Van Koppen L, et al. On (the emergence of) cyber security science and its challenges for cyber security education. In: Proceedings of the NATO IST-122 Cyber Security Science and Engineering Symposium; 13-14 October 2014; Tallinn, Estonia (Winner of the Best Paper Award)

[4] Van den Berg J. A basic set of mental models for understanding and dealing with the cybersecurity challenges of today. Journal of Information Warfare. **19**(1):26-47. Available from: https://www.jinfowar.com/journal/volume-19-issue-1/basic-set-mental-models-understanding-dealing-cybersecurity-challenges-today [Accessed: July 28, 2024]

[5] NCTV, Ministry of Justice and Security. Cyber Security Assessment Netherlands (CSAN). The Hague, The Netherlands. 2023. Available from: https://english.nctv.nl/documents/publications/2023/07/03/cyber-security-assessment-netherlands-2023 [Accessed: July 28, 2024]

[6] ISO/IEC JTC1. ISO/IEC 27001. Information Technology—Security Techniques—Information Security Management Systems—Requirements. Geneva, Switzerland: ISO; 2005

[7] Tanenbaum AS. Computer Networks. 3rd ed. New Jersey, USA: Prentice Hall; 1996. 795 p

[8] Lessig L. Code and Other Laws of Cyberspace. New York, USA: Basic Books; 1999

[9] UN International Civil Aviation Organization (ICAO). BowTieXP, bowtie methodology manual [Internet]. Revision 39. 2019. Available from: https://www.icao.int/safety/SafetyManagement/SMI/Documents/BowTieXP%20Methodology%20Manual%20v15.pdf [Accessed: July 28, 2024]

[10] Popper KR. The Open Society and its Enemies. 4th ed. Routledge & Kegan Paul Ltd; 1962. 735 p

[11] Transdisciplinarity [Internet]. Wikipedia. 2024. Available from: https://en.wikipedia.org/wiki/Transdisciplinarity [Accessed: August 6, 2024]

[12] Pelchen L. Internet users statistics in 2024 [Internet]. ForbesHOME. 2024. Available from: https://www.forbes.com/home-improvement/internet/internet-statistics/ [Accessed: July 30, 2024]

[13] Musiał K, Kazienko P. Social networks on the internet. World Wide Web. 2013;**16**:31-72. DOI: 10.1007/s11280-011-0155-z

[14] Tulane University, School of Professional Advancement. Everything you should know about the dark web [Internet]. Available from: https://sopa.tulane.edu/blog/everything-you-should-know-about-dark-web [Accessed: July 31, 2024]

[15] Atria Convergence Technologies Ltd. Top 10 uses of the internet [Internet].

2023. Available from: https://www.actcorp.in/blog/top-10-uses-of-the-internet [Accessed: July 31, 2024]

[16] CoinMarketCap. All cryptocurrencies [Internet]. 2024. Available from: https://coinmarketcap.com/all/views/all/ [Accessed: August 1, 2024]

[17] Terra J. Real-world IoT applications in 2024 [Internet]. SimpliLearn. 2024. Available from: https://www.simplilearn.com/iot-applications-article [Accessed: August 2, 2024]

[18] Bersani S. How generative AI can empower human creativity [Internet]. COLIBRYX. 2024. Available from: https://colibryx.com/en/blog/how-generative-ai-can-enhance-human-creativity

[19] Elegent Themes. What is ChatGPT & 10 creative ways to use it in 2024 [Internet]. 2024. Available from: https://www.elegantthemes.com/blog/business/what-is-chatgpt#10-generating-ai-art [Accessed: August 1, 2024]

[20] BIGCOMMERCE. 12 E-commerce trends that are powering online retail forward [Internet]. 2024. Available from: https://www.bigcommerce.com/articles/ecommerce/ecommerce-trends/ [Accessed: August 2, 2024]

[21] Chadha M. 15 cloud computing applications [Internet]. 2024. Available from: https://www.shiksha.com/online-courses/articles/cloud-computing-applications/ [Accessed: August 2, 2024]

[22] Wavetec. 2024. Available from: https://www.wavetec.com/blog/public/digitizing-public-services/ [Accessed: August 2, 2024]

[23] Abels J. Private infrastructure in geopolitical conflicts: The case of Starlink and the war in Ukraine. European Journal of International Relations. 2024. DOI: 10.1177/13540661241260653 [Accessed: August 10, 2024]

[24] Big Tech [Internet]. Wikipedia. Available from: https://en.wikipedia.org/wiki/Big_Tech [Accessed: August 10, 2024]

[25] World Economic Forum. CrowdStrike content update causes global IT outage, and other cybersecurity news to know this month [Internet]. 2024. Available from https://www.weforum.org/agenda/2024/07/crowdstrike-global-it-outage-cybersecurity-news-july-2024/ [Accessed: August 11, 2024]

[26] Stewart E. Top 10 biggest cyber attacks in history [Internet]. EM360Tech. 2024. Available from: https://em360tech.com/top-10/top-10-most-notorious-cyber-attacks-history [Accessed: August 11, 2024]

[27] Bussu A, Pulina M, Ashton S-A, Mangiarulo M. Exploring the impact of cyberbullying and cyberstalking on victims' behavioural changes in higher education during COVID-19: A case study. International Journal of Law, Crime and Justice. 2023:75. DOI: 10.1016/j.ijlcj.2023.100628 [Accessed: August 11, 2024]

[28] Raghavan R. Top 20 advantages and disadvantages of social media [Internet]. 2024. Available from: https://webandcrafts.com/blog/social-media-advantages-and-disadvantages [Accessed: August 13, 2024]

[29] Mondo Insights. Types of cyberattacks on social media & how to prevent them [Internet]. Available from: https://mondo.com/insights/social-cyberattacks/ [Accessed: August 11, 2024]

[30] Trifunović D, Zoran BZ. Cyber war—Trends and technologies. NSF Volumes.

2021;**21**:65-94. DOI: 10.37458/nstf.21.3.2 [Accessed: August 12, 2024]

[31] Bendovschi A. Cyber-attacks—Trends, patterns and security countermeasures. Procedia Economics and Finance. 2015;**28**:24-31. DOI: 10.1016/S2212-5671(15)01077-1

[32] Robinson D. US wants ASML to stop servicing China-owned chip equipment [Internet]. The Register. 2024. Available from: https://www.theregister.com/2024/03/07/us_asml_china_restrictions/ [Accessed: August 15, 2024]

[33] Concerns over Chinese involvement in 5G wireless networks [Internet]. 2024. Available from: https://en.wikipedia.org/wiki/Concerns_over_Chinese_involvement_in_5G_wireless_networks [Accessed: August 15, 2024]

[34] Internet governance [Internet]. Wikipedia. 2024. Available from: https://en.wikipedia.org/wiki/Internet_governance [Accessed: August 14, 2024]

[35] Cyber-security regulation [Internet]. Wikipedia. 2024. Available from: https://en.wikipedia.org/wiki/Cyber-security_regulation [Accessed: August 16, 2024]

[36] NCTV, Ministry of Justice and Security. The Netherlands Cybersecurity strategy 2022-2028 [Internet]. The Hague, The Netherlands. 2022. Available from: https://english.nctv.nl/documents/publications/2022/12/06/the-netherlands-cybersecurity-strategy-2022-2028 [Accessed: August 15, 2024]

[37] Husain O. 52 biggest GDPR fines and penalties (2018-2024) [Internet]. 2024. Available from: https://www.enzuzo.com/blog/biggest-gdpr-fines [Accessed: August 17, 2024]

[38] Hyperscale computing [Internet]. 2024. Available from: https://en.wikipedia.org/wiki/Hyperscale_computing [Accessed: August 20, 2024]

[39] Center for Strategic and International Studies (CSIS). Significant cyber incidents [Internet]. Available from: https://www.csis.org/programs/strategic-technologies-program/significant-cyber-incidents [Accessed: August 30, 2024]

[40] Kondruss B. Cyber attack news today [Internet]. KonBriefing. Available from: https://konbriefing.com/en-topics/cyber-attacks.html [Accessed: August 30, 2024]